TRANSFORMED BY THE TRINITY

TRANSFORMED BY THE TRINITY

*Living in the Fullness of the
Father, Son, and Holy Spirit*

☖ CAROL FRANCES JEGEN, BVM ☖

LOYOLA PRESS.
A JESUIT MINISTRY
CHICAGO

LOYOLA PRESS.
A JESUIT MINISTRY

3441 N. ASHLAND AVENUE
CHICAGO, ILLINOIS 60657
(800) 621-1008
WWW.LOYOLAPRESS.ORG

Cover image: © *The Crosiers/Gene Plaisted, OSC*
Cover design by Judine O'Shea
Interior design by Katherine Seckman Kirsch and Joan Bledig

Library of Congress Cataloging-in-Publication Data
Jegen, Carol Frances.
    Transformed by the trinity : living in the fullness of the Father, Son, and
Holy Spirit / Carol Frances Jegen.
        p. cm.
    Includes bibliographical references.
    ISBN-13: 978-0-8294-2612-0
    ISBN-10: 0-8294-2612-4
    1. Trinity. 2. Jesus Christ—Person and offices. 3. Catholic Church—
Doctrines. I. Title.
    BT111.3.J44 2008
    231'.044—dcww

2008001528

Printed in the United States of America
08 09 10 11 12 13 Versa 10 9 8 7 6 5 4 3 2 1

This book is dedicated in loving gratitude to Gerald Van Ackeren, S.J., founder of *Theology Digest*, who, in my earliest years at Marquette University's graduate program in theology, introduced me to the study of the Trinity. My gratitude extends also to each and every student in elementary, secondary, college, and graduate school who encouraged me in countless ways to share more and more understanding of our compassionate, loving God. My unspeakable gratitude goes to Corinne Hodges and Vivian Wilson, B.V.M., who generously offered to prepare this manuscript for publication, and to my sister, Mary Evelyn Jegen, S.N.D., whose invaluable suggestions enabled me to complete this study.

CONTENTS

vii

INTRODUCTION

THIS BOOK IS A RESPONSE TO my many adult students who requested more insight into the basic truth of our Christian faith: the mystery of the Blessed Trinity. Especially as Catholic Christians familiar with making the sign of the cross— "in the name of the Father, and of the Son, and of the Holy Spirit"—we are aware of our *tripersonal* God—that is, God present to us in three unique relationships. This book intends to nurture the faith of adult Christians who desire greater understanding into this beautiful mystery of God's life.

A limited understanding of any revealed mystery of our Christian faith inhibits the vibrancy and joy that God wants us to experience, even here on earth. The very word *mystery* can be misunderstood, either as some kind of detective story to be solved or as a reality accepted in "blind faith" and having little or no significance for our life this side of eternity.

The root meaning of *mystery* in the Greek language refers to a reality about which more can always be discovered. Christian faith in the Trinity was never meant to be considered simply as an unfathomable mystery. Jesus gradually revealed aspects of this beautiful reality to his disciples so that we could begin, even now in earthly existence, to enjoy our life in God. The mystery of God's tripersonal life is a reality of divine loving that is *personal*. Jesus knew by experience that participating, as a human being, in God's life would make all the difference in our lives and in the life of the world.

As we Christians of the twenty-first century ponder the significance of God's tripersonal life, we rely on two millennia of Christian reflection upon God's loving action in the lives of people. As we do so, we need to remember that there is always more to discover in the mystery of God's love for us. Each and every word and image we use is by its very nature limited in expressing the wonder of God's love.

In the earliest centuries of Christian life, tremendous controversies developed over the identities of Jesus and of the Holy Spirit. Because most of those major struggles occurred in a world of Greek thought and language, the philosophical terminology familiar in those times has not always carried the same meaning in other cultures and historical periods. Although Christians continue to refer to the Holy Spirit as the *third* person of the Blessed Trinity, who shares the divine nature of the Father and the Son, the life-giving meaning of that term is rarely conveyed to believing Christians today.

Because so many Christians do not have the philosophical background necessary to grasp the profound and beautiful insights that developed in over two millennia of our Christian history, I have relied primarily on Scripture and have included frequent references to the Church's liturgical life. Also, I have emphasized today's urgent ministries of justice and peacemaking as expressions of our sharing in God's compassion.

In this study I have preferred the word *tripersonal*, a term used by Gerald O'Collins, SJ, in *The Tripersonal God: Understanding and Interpreting the Trinity*, because it can help offset a certain subtle tritheism, a confusion about our belief in one God. When we think of the Trinity, it can be difficult to avoid thinking of God as three distinct divine persons in somewhat the same way we think of three distinct human persons. *Tripersonal* can help us focus on relational language that is so pertinent to theology that includes feminine as well as masculine images of the divine nature.

Chapter One reflects on the gift of the Holy Spirit—God's Befriending Spirit—as necessary if we are to share in God's life. God's Befriending Spirit initiates the entire process of a new creation in which new communities enable us to experience God's love. God's Befriending Spirit begins to develop a necessary prayerfulness in which we experience genuine friendship with God, a friendship that begins to make a real difference in our world.

At first sight it may seem surprising that these reflections on our tripersonal God begin with a consideration of the Holy Spirit, so often referred to as the "third" person in the Blessed Trinity. Often, Christian prayer begins with the special invocation "Come Holy Spirit," thereby inviting the Holy Spirit to be actively present. This practice indicates that we rely on the Holy Spirit's active presence as we pray.

Chapter Two focuses on four descriptive names given to Jesus in the Gospels. Each of these names—Beloved Son, Servant, Word Made Flesh, and Lamb of God—gives us profound insight into how Jesus expressed, in unique ways, God's life and love for us. Because of our oneness with Jesus, we can see more clearly how we, too, are meant to participate in this divine life.

Chapter Three considers God the Father—Jesus' own Abba and ours. This chapter relies heavily on Jesus' long conversation with his disciples at the Last Supper (John 14–17). At that time he explains more clearly the relationship that he enjoys with God the Father and that he extends to us who are his friends.

Chapter Four considers more extensively some of what it means that we are able to share God's life through, with, and in Jesus.

Chapter Five explores what it means that the "new creation" really takes place as we share God's tripersonal life evermore faithfully in today's suffering world.

As we move into this new millennium, sometimes the power of evil can seem overwhelming as we face threats of terrorism, military buildup, and increasing worldwide poverty and destitution. More than ever we need a meaningful, faith-filled understanding of God's continual, compassionate love. God has invited us to be a part of divine, loving work in the world. This book can help us understand more clearly how we are meant to participate in that active, restorative love.

A steady, ongoing prayerfulness on our part is necessary to enjoy this divine life. This book can help us nurture such a process. Suggestions for prayerful reflection are given at the end of each chapter. A brief bibliography is included for those who want to pursue more extensive study.

☙ 1 ☙

The Befriending Spirit

*"To carry forward the work of Christ under the
lead of the befriending Spirit."*
—Gaudium et Spes

In its Pastoral Constitution on the Church,
Gaudium et Spes (Joy and Hope), the Second Vatican
Council gave us a special title for the Holy Spirit; namely,
the "befriending Spirit" (GS 3). In this major Council document concerned with the impact of the Church in today's
world, this somewhat surprising title for the Holy Spirit is
highly significant. What are some of the reasons "befriending" is a particularly meaningful way to describe the greatly
needed action of God at this time in human history? How
can "befriending" help us experience and understand more
of God's desire to share life with us?

"Befriending" means that we make friends and become
friends with each other. Friends relate to one another in
understanding and loving ways. Friendship demands freedom, the freedom of each friend to give and to receive love.

A forced friend is an impossibility simply because love cannot be forced. One of the great joys of genuine friendship is the realization of love freely given and received. Within the relationships of true friendship, each person recognizes and appreciates the goodness and gifts of the other.

"Befriending Spirit" is the most beautiful way to describe the personal action of the divine person whom we Christians refer to as the Holy Spirit. The Gospel of Luke gives particular prominence to the Holy Spirit as the one whose action is necessary to initiate Christian life—a life of genuine friendship with God and with other people.

In Luke's Gospel, the Annunciation account makes it undeniably clear that without the gift of God's Befriending Spirit, the incarnation of God's own Son could not happen. Luke emphasizes also that Mary's openness to receiving the Befriending Spirit was absolutely necessary (Luke 1:26–38).

Luke informs us that even before Mary received the special gift of God's Befriending Spirit, that same Holy Spirit was promised to Zachariah's son John. "He will be filled with the holy Spirit even from his mother's womb" (1:15). Elizabeth, inspired by the Holy Spirit, greeted Mary in joy, as did Elizabeth's child John, when he leapt within her womb (1:41–42). After John's birth, Zachariah, "filled with the holy Spirit" proclaimed his prophetic canticle (1:67). Later when Simeon saw the child Jesus in the temple, the Holy Befriending Spirit enabled this "righteous and devout" elderly man to recognize Jesus as God's specially anointed (2:25–32). In his entire story of Jesus' birth and early life, Luke emphasizes again and again that new life with God can come to us only through the initiative of God's Befriending Spirit.

At the end of Luke's Gospel, Jesus' disciples were told to wait for the gift of God's Befriending Spirit, the promise of Jesus' Father (24:49). Without this Holy Spirit, these followers of Jesus could do nothing. The first five chapters of the Acts of the Apostles portray the tremendous change in these disciples when they received the Befriending Spirit at Pentecost. In both Luke's Gospel and in Acts, the giving and receiving of the Holy Spirit is the necessary new beginning of God's life-giving action in the world.

At the beginning of this new millennium, as we recall the beginning of Jesus' life and the beginning of the Church's life, it can be very meaningful to remember that the Holy Spirit is also the *Befriending Spirit*. When John XXIII called the Second Vatican Council, he emphasized that the initiative in calling such a major event in the life of the Church was an inspiration of the Holy Spirit. At the time, no one envisioned precisely how the Council would bring new life into the Church. Nor was the Holy Spirit referred to as the Befriending Spirit. But now, close to half a century after John XXIII's prophetic call, the special title of *Befriending Spirit* takes on greater significance.

One of the great surprises of Vatican II was the document *Gaudium et Spes* (Joy and Hope), often referred to as *The Church in the Modern World*. This document was not part of the original plan of the Council but came about at the insistence of those bishops from poorer countries wherein two-thirds of the world's people live, often in dire poverty.

This document is addressed to "the whole of humanity" (GS 2), and speaks to the crucial issues facing today's world. Its introductory statement is a prophetic challenge. "The joys and the hopes, the griefs and the anxieties of the men of this age, especially those who are poor or in any way afflicted, these are the joys and hopes, the griefs and anxieties of the followers of Christ. Indeed, nothing genuinely human fails to raise an echo in their hearts" (GS 1).

In response to this worldwide urgency, the befriending Spirit is highlighted as leading the way for the entire Church (GS 3). At this period of human history, perhaps no other title of the Holy Spirit could carry the significance of God's compassionate action in our lives with greater meaning than the name *befriending*.[1]

Befriending can happen on a personal, community, or national level. On a personal level, befriending implies recognition of another person's goodness and worth. When befriending extends to a community, the value of the community is appreciated. Befriending on the national level often implies action in response to some critical need. In *Gaudium et Spes* the act of befriending is highlighted on the national level in response to the suffering of the whole world's poor and afflicted. Wherever God's Befriending Spirit is acting—in a personal, community, or national context—the action is always a gift.

God's Gift to Us

When one friend gives a gift to another friend, thoughtful care goes into the selection of that gift. The one friend chooses something that will convey the understanding and love between the two friends. Likewise, the friend receiving the gift must receive it in a loving way, or it ceases to be a gift. Receiving a gift in grateful love is just as necessary as giving a gift in genuine love.

One experience made a lasting impression on me regarding gifts and friendship. One of my students received a gift package from a former friend who had offended her. At the time, the student was not ready to forgive the person who had sent the package. Consequently, the offended student decided to throw the package into Lake Michigan. I don't know if the broken friendship was ever restored, but certainly the rejected package could not be considered a gift. It had not been received but was, rather, rejected and destroyed.

When the Befriending Spirit is sent by the risen Jesus and his Father (Luke 24:49 and John 15:26), the loving friendship between Jesus and his disciples is made possible. At the Last Supper on the night before Jesus died, how strongly he insisted, "I have called you friends, because I have told you everything I have heard from my Father" (John 15:15). Jesus knew that his gift of the Befriending Spirit was absolutely necessary for the reign of God's love to come about. No wonder Jesus insisted that his disciples remain in Jerusalem for the gift of "power from on high." There was no other way they could share the good news of God's redeeming love without the gift of God's Befriending Spirit (Luke 24:44–49).

As a friendship matures, friends continue to exchange gifts. Each time a gift is given, the love between the friends is strengthened. In the fourth chapter of Acts, we read of a Pentecost experience wherein the community was given the needed strength in a difficult time. After their arrest, when Peter and John returned to the community and joined them in grateful prayer, once again "they were all filled with the holy Spirit and continued to speak the word of God with boldness" (Acts 4:31).

Imagine if the disciples had refused that gift? Then imagine our own situation today when we ignore the Befriending Spirit and refuse the gifts offered to us for our own good and the good of the world? It is necessary that we recognize and accept joyfully the gift of the Befriending Spirit from Jesus and God the Father.

God continues to offer us the gift of the Befriending Spirit. The Second Vatican Council is referred to often as a "New Pentecost." Each of us receives the Holy Spirit at baptism and confirmation. Without this gift of the Holy Spirit, the Befriending Spirit, we cannot live the Christian life and have a friendship with God. Without the Spirit's help, we could not respond with a maturing Christianity.

Because the Holy Spirit continues to be given as the Befriending Spirit, vital friendship is involved, not only with God but also with our sisters and brothers in God's human family. In fact, this special gift of God's Befriending Spirit is necessary for each and every human person to find meaning and genuine happiness in life. Loving relationships are necessary in all human groupings, from the smallest families to the largest nations. Only when we receive the gift of God's Befriending Spirit can we begin to realize the heartfelt longings for justice and peace that grow naturally out of our love for friend and neighbor.

Making New Creation Possible

One of the most beautiful ways of describing the gift of God's Befriending Spirit is that of beginning a new creation. The Befriending Spirit is the vehicle to this new creation. The final chapters of Isaiah proclaimed God's intent "to create new heavens / and a new earth" (65:17). Centuries later, in John's Gospel, when Jesus explained new birth to Nicodemus, he said that life would come through "water and Spirit" (3:5–8). In writing to the Galatians, Paul insisted that what really mattered was "a new creation" (6:15). In Scripture, the Spirit is often referred to in relation to this new creation.

Such cosmic implications of the Befriending Spirit's coming have special relevance in our part of human history when a new creation is so desperately needed. Ecological concerns continue to mount as natural resources such as rain forests are devastated and the life-threatening dangers of air pollution increase. Seemingly endless wars and the projected militarization of outer space gives even greater urgency to the dire need for the Spirit's beginning a new creation. Isaiah's prophecy of "new heavens and a new earth" did not envision the life-threatening situations of the twenty-first century. Nor did the final chapters of the book of Revelation in describing "a new heaven and a new earth" (21:1). Probably, most persons who are making day-to-day efforts of response to our ecological needs and needs for peace and justice in the world are not aware of Scripture's promise of a new heaven and a new earth. But those people are genuinely concerned about today's serious challenges and are taking appropriate actions as best they can, even in very small ways. Such efforts of befriending our earth are witness to the quiet, steady promptings of the Befriending Spirit and the Spirit's mission of a new creation.

In the beginning, "a mighty wind" swept over the waters when God created heaven and earth (Genesis 1:1–2). As the creation story continues, it becomes increasingly clear that this mighty wind, this "breath of God," was and still is necessary for all the creatures of God's earth to exist. The Befriending Spirit is vital to our survival and to the renewal of creation.

Creating a Loving Atmosphere

Atmosphere is a descriptive term referring to an environment and whether or not it is conducive for the flourishing of life. Sometimes *atmosphere* is used to describe a living situation, such as a building, a home, a school, a meeting place, or a city. In *Enjoying God's Beauty*, John Navone reminds us that the gift of the Spirit enables and empowers us to see and delight in the beauty of God in our human life story.[2] The Befriending Spirit is vital to creating a good atmosphere. Paradoxically so, a good and loving atmosphere is needed for accepting God's gift of the Spirit.

Loving atmospheres are extremely important for ongoing friendship. Sometimes friends are quite involved in creating life-giving atmospheres in which genuine love can be expressed. We can spend hours sometimes in designing and bestowing artifacts of beauty to enhance the quality of life. But the most essential aspect of a beautiful life-giving atmosphere is the intangible quality of love that permeates the structures in which we live.

Loving atmospheres can be very poor as far as material possessions are concerned. And elegant possessions do not guarantee an atmosphere conducive to friendship. No matter the amount of material possessions, loving atmospheres are basic for human life to thrive. Even a smile or a frown can make a tremendous difference in the atmosphere of a place. Sometimes I wonder if another descriptive title for the Holy Spirit might be the *Smile of God*. Smiles are given even before words are spoken between friends. They are vital to creating a loving atmosphere anywhere.

Two ministry experiences have helped me realize the importance of smiles. In ministry to farm workers, especially in California, the language is usually Spanish. In my earliest days of ministry with them, I was not familiar with Spanish. Smiles were our primary means of communication; with them we spoke the language of loving, active concern.

In prison ministry, smiles have helped change a drab and sometimes heartless atmosphere. One recent experience strengthened my awareness of the importance of smiles. After waiting for almost two hours, a friend and I were finally taken to the visiting room. I'll never forget the radiant smile of our prisoner friend as we entered. In both situations, smiles spoke more than a thousand words.

Loving atmospheres, simple and poor as they may be, are beautiful because they participate in the creative power of God. We can hardly reflect on the wonder of God's creation without becoming more aware of how beautiful

God's created universe really is. In the new creation begun by God's Befriending Spirit, we are empowered to grow in appreciation of God's beauty, which always attracts us to move forward in life-giving ways.

Often, in amazing ways, we find ourselves involved in beautifying our living situations, sometimes simply with a flower in an unexpected place. Several years ago when I was involved in inner-city ministry, I remember a young child running home with one dandelion held tightly and carefully in his small hand. I was amazed that he'd found a flower in his empty, muddy, forsaken surroundings, hardly an atmosphere of caring love. Probably, he was running home to give this gift to his mother. His face really glowed with delight. I imagined his mother receiving the gift with a smile of grateful joy. Surely, the Befriending Spirit was active there.

Loving atmospheres are intrinsic to the nurturing of life-giving friendships. In creating such an atmosphere, God's Befriending Spirit is always at work. Regardless of the material circumstances, the Holy Spirit begins to infuse a spirit of active, loving concern necessary to transform situations so that friendship with God and with one another can begin and thrive. We need to be open to receive this gift.

Forming Caring Communities

A most basic human need is to belong—to be nurtured within a caring community. Isolation, neglect, and abandonment can be excruciating sufferings, often intensified tragically by frustration, hopelessness, and violence. Because we are made in the image and likeness of God (Genesis 1:26), we are designed to enjoy God's own community, the tripersonal life of divine loving. No wonder our human experiences of loving concern are so crucial! No wonder God's Befriending Spirit works tirelessly to form such communities in all human situations. At the very heart of the new creation process is the formation of caring communities.

The creative action of our Befriending Spirit continually influences the formation of new communities in which we can experience God's love. One of the most promising developments in the Vatican II era has been the formation of small Christian communities throughout the world.[3] Whether these communities were formed among the poor of Latin America, Asia, or Africa or among the relatively affluent of North America and Europe, the Befriending Spirit has nurtured a prayerfulness that inspires action for justice and peace. Members of these small Christian communities give ongoing witness to the challenge expressed in the opening statement of *Gaudium et Spes*: "Indeed, nothing genuinely human fails to raise an echo in their hearts" (GS 1).

Community formation created through the action of the Befriending Spirit takes many forms as we face the critical needs of the world of today and tomorrow. *Gaudium et Spes* devotes an entire chapter to "The Community of [Hu]mankind." This discussion of community precedes the treatment of the major challenges and concerns facing us today. In chapter 3, "Human Activity throughout the World," we are reminded that "God is preparing a new dwelling place and a new earth where justice will abide, and whose blessedness will answer and surpass all the longings for peace which spring up in the human heart" (GS 39).

The preface of part 2 of this document lists some problems of special urgency facing the Church: "marriage and the family, human progress, life in its economic, social and political dimensions, the bonds between the family of nations, and peace" (GS 46). How significant that the final chapter is entitled "The Fostering of Peace and the Promotion of a Community of Nations." Encouraging honest dialogue, the concluding section highlights the Church's mission "to unify under one Spirit all [people] of whatever nation, race or culture" (GS 92).

When Luke described the Pentecost event in the first two chapters of Acts, he emphasized the communal experience of Jesus' disciples and of the people of many nations who were assembled there and were "filled with the holy Spirit" (2:4). In summary fashion at the end of the second chapter, Luke described the key characteristics of the Spirit-filled community: "They devoted themselves to teaching of the apostles and to the communal life, to the breaking of the bread and to the prayers" (2:42). Luke also commented on how these believers "had all things in common," even selling "their property and possessions and divid[ing] them among all according to each one's need" (2:44–45).

These community descriptions in Acts emphasize faithful, steadfast prayer, enabling the Befriending Spirit's new creative power to work. Thus, in prayer, we can ask for a new outpouring of God's Befriending Spirit, so that loving communities can continue being created.

Invited through Our Prayerfulness

Luke makes it clear that Mary's prayerful witness was significant in preparing Christ's followers to receive God's Befriending Spirit at Pentecost. "Together they devoted themselves to constant prayer. There were some women in their company, and Mary the mother of Jesus and his brothers" (Acts 1:14). Previously, in the Nativity story of his Gospel, Luke had highlighted Mary's openness to God. Twice Luke inserted statements emphasizing Mary's prayer, particularly in situations where unexpected happenings had occurred. Surely it was surprising that the first visitors arriving to greet her newborn son, Jesus, were rugged shepherds from the nearby fields (2:15–20). Luke described Mary's reaction. "Mary treasured all these things and reflected on them in her heart" (2:19).

The second time Luke highlights Mary's open, prayerful attitude comes at the end of the Infancy Narrative. When Mary and Joseph brought the infant Jesus to the temple, Simeon warned Mary that she would suffer intensely because her child would be rejected by many (Luke 2:34–35). The chapter concludes with the heart-rending experience of Mary and Joseph when Jesus was lost for three days. In response to these sufferings, Luke tells us, "His mother meanwhile kept all these things in memory" (2:51).

Luke highlights Mary's prayerfulness as treasuring all these things and reflecting on them in her heart as well as keeping all these things in memory. These references to Mary's prayerfulness are preceded in the first chapter of his Gospel, in which Luke introduces Mary as a woman overshadowed and empowered by the Holy Spirit (1:35). God's Befriending Spirit nurtured Mary's life of prayerful intimacy with God, especially in times when strong faith in God's love was needed. Out of her own experience Mary was able later to nurture the prayer life of the Church as it was empowered by the Holy Spirit, especially in the face of new challenges.

The ongoing history of the Church bears witness to a deep conviction of the Befriending Spirit's necessary and active presence in the prayer life of Christians. Time and again, Christians begin prayer with an invocation to the Holy Spirit for enlightenment and guidance. *Veni Sancte Spiritu* (Come Holy Spirit) is a familiar invocation, now made more familiar through the various Taizé chants sung in prayer groups large and small.[4]

In Paul's Letter to the Ephesians, those early Christians were encouraged to "be filled with the Spirit, addressing one another in psalms and hymns and inspired songs" (5:18–19). In his letter to the Romans, Paul stressed the necessity of the Spirit's continual help in the prayer life of the Christian community:

> In the same way, the Spirit too comes to the aid of our weakness; for we do not know how to pray as we ought, but the Spirit itself intercedes with inexpressible groanings. And the one who searches hearts knows what is the intention of the Spirit, because it intercedes for the holy ones according to God's will. (8:26–27)

Undoubtedly, as a fervent Jew, Paul was familiar with the Servant Songs in Isaiah, those powerful readings that the Church now prays every year during Holy Week (Isaiah 42:1–7; 49:1–6; 50:4–9a; 52:13—53:12). In all these Scripture texts, prayer, initiated and guided by the Holy Spirit, strengthens the followers of God especially in times of suffering.[5]

The first verse of the first Servant Song sings of the gift of God's Spirit, "Here is my servant whom I uphold, / my chosen one with whom I am pleased, / Upon whom I have put my spirit" (Isaiah 42:1). As the songs continue, the necessary prayerfulness of this servant, who is prophet par excellence, is given greater and greater prominence. The second song pictures the servant resting in hidden ways with God before the words and actions of the Spirit-filled person and community could become "light to the nations" (49:2–3, 6). The third song testifies to the prophet-servant's habitual prayerfulness as "morning after morning" God strengthens this servant, especially in times of suffering (50:4). The fourth and final song begins with the word "See," an invitation to contemplate God's compassionate love in the midst of the servant's excruciating sufferings (52:13).

In our time, Karl Rahner's term *self-communication* can give helpful insight into the Befriending Spirit's role in our life of prayer.[6] In our experience of genuine friendship, we know the necessity of taking time to "talk things over." We reveal, or communicate, our true selves to one another. There is really no meaning to friendship if the two friends don't communicate honestly. The Holy Spirit develops within us this ability as our friendship with God deepens.

The Befriending Spirit is also called the Spirit of Love.[7] No action of God in relation to us can be anything other than an expression of love because "God is love" (1 John 4:16). Thus, when the Befriending Spirit acts within us, the result is love—in relation to God and with one another.

Helping Us to Pray

This action of the Spirit is described by Stanislaus Lyonnet in *The Christian Lives by the Spirit.*

> The Spirit teaches what Jesus taught, but causes it to enter into our hearts. There is, therefore, a perfect continuity in revelation: coming from the Father, it is communicated to us by the Son, but it attains its fullness when it enters into the most intimate part of our being through the action of the Spirit.[8]

Whenever and wherever Christians gather together to celebrate the Eucharist, special prayer to the Holy Spirit is voiced. The Befriending Spirit's unifying power echoes throughout these major Eucharistic Prayers:

- Eucharistic Prayer II: "May all of us who share in the body and blood of Christ be brought together in unity by the Holy Spirit."

- Eucharistic Prayer III: The Holy Spirit's power in Mary's virginal conception of Jesus is proclaimed. Often we are reminded that "by the working of the Holy Spirit," "all life, all holiness comes."

- Eucharistic Prayer III: "Grant that we, who are nourished by his body and blood, may be filled with his Holy Spirit, and become one body, one spirit in Christ."

- Eucharistic Prayer IV: Many times we recall the risen Jesus' gift of the Holy Spirit "that we might live no longer for ourselves but for him" as we "complete his work on earth."

As we ponder these Eucharistic Prayers, which are at the very heart of the Church's prayer life, we can appreciate more fully how the Holy Spirit is truly the Befriending Spirit. This Spirit of God's love continually transforms us who receive Jesus' body and blood to become genuine friends of God and of one another. As Navone comments, "The mutual love/friendship of the Eucharistic community is the sacrament of God's beauty, revealing the splendor and communicating the joy of God's love to the world."[9]

The more we become aware of the Holy Spirit's action in our lives, the more we will appreciate why the Second Vatican Council emphasized the Spirit's befriending role. As we become more aware of the horrendous divisiveness and violence in our world today, we realize an unprecedented urgency for "renewing the face of the earth." This new creation can come about only as we continue to receive—and be formed by—God's Befriending Spirit. This Spirit enables us to become genuine friends of God and thus with one another.

Questions for Reflection

1. Who are your trusted friends and why? Name what you consider key attributes to a healthy friendship.

2. How do you imagine the Befriending Spirit being involved with your life right now?

3. How would you describe a loving atmosphere? What have you done or said at times to create a more loving atmosphere for others?

4. What do you think the Befriending Spirit brings into a situation that helps people experience God's presence?

5. Reflect on Luke's comments regarding Mary's open, prayerful spirit. In what ways is your life similar to Mary's, and in what ways is it different?

6. How are prayer and conversation similar? When do you most sense that you are in conversation with God and with other people?

⚛ 2 ⚛

Jesus

"I call you friends."
—John 15:15

O
NE OF JESUS' MOST PROFOUNDLY BEAUTIFUL
statements in John's Gospel expresses his desire
to be intimate friends with his followers. "I have
called you friends, because I have told you everything I have
heard from my Father" (15:15).

It is not surprising that the Gospels give different names
for Jesus, endearing names that attempt to express something
of the relationship Jesus has with his friends. It is impossible
to fully comprehend the meanings of Jesus' various names.
But we will concentrate on four of them and how they define
our relationship with him: Beloved Son, Servant, Word, and
Lamb of God. Each of these names can help clarify what it
means for humans to share God's life.

The Infancy Narratives (stories of Jesus' birth) of
Matthew's and Luke's Gospels inform us that Mary's son is to
be named Jesus. In Matthew's Gospel, the angel of the Lord

tells Joseph, who is engaged to Mary, "She will bear a son and you are to name him Jesus, because he will save his people from their sins" (Matthew 1:21). In Luke's Gospel, the angel Gabriel tells Mary, "You will conceive in your womb and bear a son, and you shall name him Jesus." Also, Gabriel informs Mary that Jesus will be called "Son of the Most High" and "Son of God" (Luke 1:31–32, 35). Matthew concludes the angel's message to Joseph with a most significant reference to the prophet Isaiah: "'The virgin shall be with child and bear a son, / and they shall name him Emmanuel,' / which means 'God is with us'" (Matthew 1:23, quoting Isaiah 7:14).

Both Infancy Narratives give "Jesus" as the proper name for Mary's child and also indicate Jesus' special relationship with God, a God who is always with us to save us from sin—anything and everything that can keep us from enjoying a life of friendship with God. No wonder Luke highlights Mary's great joy as she hastened to bring this news to Elizabeth and exclaimed, "My soul proclaims the greatness of the Lord; my spirit rejoices in God my savior" (Luke 1:46–47). Truly, Mary was echoing Gabriel's first word to her in his profound greeting, "Hail, favored one! The Lord is with you" (Luke 1:28).

Beloved Son

In Matthew and Luke's stories of Jesus' birth, the fact that he is called Son of the Most High, Son of God, and Emmanuel indicates a special relationship between Jesus and God—it is a *family* relationship. In some mysterious way, Jesus' relationship with God indicates that we, too, can share life with God as we would share life in a loving family.

All three Synoptic Gospels—Matthew, Mark, and Luke—in describing the baptism of Jesus, add the word "beloved" in recounting God's voice speaking from heaven (Matthew 3:17; Mark 1:11; Luke 3:22). Mark and Luke add a special personal touch by way of God's speaking with Jesus: "*You* are my beloved Son; with *you* I am well pleased" (Mark 1:11 and Luke 3:22, italics added).

This same name, Beloved Son, is repeated in the Transfiguration accounts of Matthew 17:5 and Mark 9:7—when Jesus' appearance changed and three of his disciples saw him speaking with Moses and the prophet Elijah. Luke identifies Jesus as God's "chosen Son" (9:35). All three Gospels include God's words to those disciples who witnessed this event: "Listen to him."

Each Synoptic account of the Transfiguration describes Israel's prophetic leaders Moses and Elijah conversing with Jesus. For the early Christians familiar with their Jewish Scriptures, Moses and Elijah were prophets who knew from experience that only a prayerful union with God could sustain them. These great prophets were known as friends of God and witnesses to the Wisdom testimony, "She produces friends of God and prophets" (Wisdom 7:27).

One of the most revealing stories of Moses' friendship with God is found in Exodus: "The LORD used to speak to Moses face to face, as one man speaks to another" (33:11). When Moses became fearful and even despondent about continuing his leadership role in the Exodus, a very honest dialogue with God took place. Moses reminded God that there was no hope for the ongoing journey unless God continued to accompany them. How strengthening was the Lord's response to Moses! "This request, too, which you have just made, I will carry out, because you have found favor with me and you are my intimate friend" (33:17).

This prophetic intimacy with God is intensified in the words *Beloved Son*. No other name for Jesus expresses more clearly the very sharing of God's divine life than this title, which expresses a parent-child relationship. It is a greater relationship than that of God and any other person, be it Moses or Elijah.

Pondering the meaning of Beloved Son as a name for Jesus brings us to an important consideration of how we share in God's life. The relation of child to parent is first of all one of receiving life. No one can be called father or mother if there is no son or daughter. In our human experience, receptivity of life is just as essential as the giving of life. New human life is meant to come into existence as an expression of genuine love.

The Nicene Creed of Christian faith professes our belief in "one Lord, Jesus Christ, the only Son of God, eternally begotten of the Father, God from God, Light from Light, true God from true God, begotten, not made, one in Being with the Father." As the Father's only-begotten Beloved Son, from all eternity this Son is receiving the divine life of the Father. This receiving is not "inferior" or "secondary" in the relationship. If Jesus had not received this life from God and lived it in our presence, we would have no intelligible concept of God's tripersonal nature.

In God, this only-begotten sonship transcends our human masculinity and femininity, but it does indicate the importance of receptivity in our human relationships. Made in the image and likeness of God (Genesis 1:27), we can experience both the giving and the receiving of life. We can know by experience that receiving is essential and in no way inferior.

Both giving and receiving of love are necessary for us in our human friendships with one another and, above all, with God. We can't begin to comprehend the mystery of God's giving life to us. Even more incomprehensible is that God receives love from us because of our oneness in Jesus, God's Beloved Son.

Servant

In chapter 1, we saw how God's Befriending Spirit played such a key role in the life of prayer. The necessity of the Spirit's influence in prayer was indicated briefly in the context of the Servant Songs in the book of Isaiah. These texts, which are inserted in both the Baptism and Transfiguration texts of the Synoptic Gospels, are direct references to the prophet-servant theology of the second part of Isaiah, chapters 40–55.[1] When Mark, Matthew, and Luke rephrase the introductory statement of the first Servant Song (Isaiah 42:1) by replacing the name Servant with the name Beloved Son, not only are they sounding a keynote for the entire prophet-servant theology, which culminates in the final song of the Suffering Servant (Isaiah 52:13—53:12), but they are also indicating that the Servant of Yahweh presented in Isaiah finds fulfillment in Jesus, the Beloved Son of God.

In many cultures today, including that of the United States, the word *servant* hardly conveys the meaning designated in Isaiah. Today it usually implies a person who performs certain tasks, often menial ones. Probably, the author of Isaiah would have used the word *slave* to describe a person in that role.[2]

Actually the Greek word *pais*, used in the translation from the original Hebrew, carries the meaning of both servant and child.[3] Beyond these linguistic clarifications we can find a beautiful clarification of the love relationship characteristic of the Isaian Servant, who is truly a beloved son in whom Yahweh delights (Isaiah 42:1).

The final Servant Song begins with, "See, my servant shall prosper, / he shall be raised high and greatly exalted" (Isaiah 52:13). The Gentiles, those who do not share Israel's faith in a compassionate God, conclude that this person was "smitten by God and afflicted" (Isaiah 53:4). Yahweh's response to this suffering person's condition was quite different.

> Through his suffering, my servant shall justify many,
>   and their guilt he shall bear. . . .
> Because he surrendered himself to death
>   and was counted among the wicked;
> And he shall take away the sins of many,
>   and win pardon for their offenses.
>   —Isaiah 53:11–12

This Servant was not smitten by God and afflicted. Quite the contrary. This Servant had been engulfed in the depths of human anguish and suffering caused by human sin. This Servant had brought the power of God's compassionate love and had completely transformed the sinful situation.

The writer of the Gospel of Luke and the Acts of the Apostles gives special prominence to this prophet-servant theology. When Jesus entered the Nazareth synagogue to begin his public ministry, he opened the scroll of Isaiah and identified himself as the prophet-servant of Yahweh (Luke 4:21). The scroll of Isaiah read:

> The Spirit of the Lord is upon me,
>   because he has anointed me
>   to bring glad tidings to the poor.
> He has sent me to proclaim liberty to captives
>   and recovery of sight to the blind,
>   to let the oppressed go free,
> and to proclaim a year acceptable to the Lord.[4]
>   —Luke 4:18–19, quoting Isaiah 61:1–2

The entire ministry of Jesus is presented in this context of Isaiah's prophet-servant. The poor would hear glad tidings; captives would be freed; the blind would see; prisoners would be released.

Luke also tells us that Jesus' message was rejected because "no prophet is accepted in his own native place" (Luke 4:24). Jesus' own townspeople, lacking faith in him, expelled him from the synagogue and even tried to kill him (4:28–30).

From the very beginning of his public life, Jesus knew the rejection and persecution of Yahweh's prophet-servant.

In the first five chapters of Acts, in which we read about the experience of the earliest Christian community of Jerusalem, it is not surprising that Jesus is named Servant, a name that had tremendous meaning for those first Jewish Christians. After Peter cured a man crippled from birth, he then assured the astonished crowd that this healing power was not his own. Peter proclaimed boldly, "The God of Abraham, [the God] of Isaac, and [the God] of Jacob, the God of our ancestors, has glorified his servant Jesus" (3:13).

As the early Christian community moved more and more into the Gentile world, the identification of Jesus as Servant of Yahweh became deemphasized because of cultural reasons not unlike our own.[5] In Greek and Roman culture the word *servant* carried meanings of inferiority, even of slavery. However, in our times, Salvadorian Jesuit Jon Sobrino has emphasized the need to highlight Jesus as the Suffering Servant of Yahweh.[6] In light of the terrible sufferings and persecutions of the world's poor, this name for Jesus can convey life-giving hope, especially in the midst of death-dealing circumstances.

Sobrino has also identified poverty-stricken peoples of the world as the suffering servant. In an essay entitled "The Crucified Peoples: Yahweh's Suffering Servant Today," Sobrino intersperses texts from the fourth Servant Song (Isaiah 52:13—53:12) with descriptions of the Salvadoran people and others who are suffering cruel opposition and martyrdom at the usually hidden hands of the world's affluent countries.[7] But like the Servant Jesus, crucified and risen, these contemporary martyrs witness to forgiveness and hope in the promise of new life.

In the prayer of the early persecuted community recorded in Acts 4:23–30, the servant was called God's *holy* Servant. For those first Jewish Christians, the word *holy* indicated a privileged relationship with God, who is called holy. The prayer of the early community as recorded in Acts 4 highlights the compassion of God, a "suffering-with" God.[8] Perhaps no other name for Jesus expresses God's compassionate love more clearly than the name Holy Servant Jesus.

Our oneness with Jesus today calls us to share life with him in a special way, living out the attitude of Holy Servant whose compassion for the poor led him to give his very life. Especially in life-threatening circumstances, followers of Jesus need to recall his prophetic promise to those who would share his life as friends: "In the world you will have trouble, but take courage, I have conquered the world" (John 16:33).

Word Made Flesh

John's Gospel does not begin with an Infancy Narrative but introduces Jesus as the Word of God become flesh (1:14). In the beginning this Word existed, and this Word was in God's presence. This Word was God (1:1–2). Nothing can exist apart from this Word (1:3).

Those who exist in union with the Word of God find life to enlighten everyone (John 1:4). Those who live in union with this Word of God are empowered to become children of God (1:12), an endearing way to speak of those who share God's very life as intimate friends.

John's Gospel also describes the Word made flesh as dwelling among us, another beautiful way to speak of the personal presence friends hope to enjoy as much as possible. In this context of God's being with us, we are able to see "the glory as of the Father's only Son, / full of grace and truth" and that "grace and truth came through Jesus Christ" (1:14, 17). How clearly this prologue identifies God's glory with God's enduring love that is beautifully manifest and experienced, especially in Jesus.

Being the oldest child in our family, I can remember the delight of my mother and father when my younger brother or sisters spoke their first words. For some time, that word was preceded by a smile and by different little gurgling sounds that were the first signs of recognition and response. But those early attempts to communicate never brought forth a joyous response equal to the utterance of the baby's first actual word.

Surely in those days, neither my parents nor any one of us in the family were familiar with Karl Rahner's descriptive phrase "self-communication."[9] But we did know that this little child was a person who was beginning to find a way to respond to human love by speaking a word. By means of the baby's first word, and all the words that followed, this little child was sharing his or her very self.

In these days of ever greater technological means of communicating, sometimes the personal aspect of self-communication is slighted if not lost altogether. Many times e-mail takes care of our communication needs without any visible personal encounter. Each day we are inundated, and often overwhelmed, by print material—newspapers, e-mail, and so on—without much, if any, personal encounter. It can be a real challenge to remember that words are meant to be expressions of personal caring and concern, of genuine self-communication.

Rahner's use of the term *self-communication* with respect to God can challenge us to consider more prayerfully the prologue of John's Gospel. In human experience, when words of love are spoken, the union of love is strengthened and made more beautiful. This deepening of union occurs between two persons and also in a community context, including a family and a wider Church or civic community. As Thompson reminds us:

> Holy Writ never presents us with an isolated Jesus. It is a Jesus forming and being formed by a community of disciples: his Mother Mary, the apostles and other followers, forming a sort of inner and intimate circle, and then a Jesus moving outward to others.[10]

Jesus, God's Word made flesh, really communicates God's Self to us and leads us to a new awareness of God's tripersonal life. Somehow, this Word, who is God, was "in the beginning" expressing the glory, grace, and truth of the Father and his only-begotten Son (John 1:2, 14). In the fullness of time when this Word became flesh, the entire human family was able to enter a new, loving communing with God.[11]

In considering what it means to share God's life, perhaps we should use the term *communing* rather than *communicating*. Communing can offset some of the impersonal character of a culture that has become so technical. When we use the term *communing*, it's easier to think about how personally we can receive words spoken in genuine love.[12] Communing may help us realize something of God's tripersonal life as we share in that life more fully through, with, and in Jesus, the Word who was with God in the beginning and who is now made flesh.

In our human language patterns, prepositions indicate relationships. When John's Gospel tells us that the Word was *with* God, that Gospel is proclaiming a wondrous relationship as intrinsic to God's very life. That Gospel is proclaiming that God cannot be God without expressing the Word of enduring love.

Long before God's Word was revealed to us in Jesus, the prophet announced that God's special presence would be *with* us because a virgin's child would be called Emmanuel, meaning "God with us." John's Gospel continues that idea of "God with us" in explaining that Jesus, who is God with us, has been with God from the very beginning. In fact, Jesus—as the Word—is an expression of God to us. We can enter a loving relationship with God because—by nature—God is relational.

The beginning of John's Gospel reveals that this Word of God made flesh is the eternal Beloved Son, who as Word manifests the Father's glory, the Father's enduring love. Here we learn that a human personal encounter with

Jesus gives us "access to God's very own triune Self."[13] This Gospel also makes very clear that we share in this life of divine love by freely accepting that love and that relationship. John 1:11 makes the tragic statement: "his own people did not accept him."

Another important theme of this Gospel's first chapter is the creative power of God beginning a "new creation." Not only was the Befriending Spirit involved in the new creation, but "in the beginning" all things were made by this Word who is with God (John 1:1–3). Those who receive this creative Word now become God's children, sharing God's life. A new creative power is present in the world in Jesus and in those who receive him. As Thompson reminds us, Jesus "keeps us aware of something much greater and more ultimate than even being freed from sin, namely, the beauty of union with God."[14]

In *History and the Triune God*, the theologian Jürgen Moltmann emphasizes new creation not only for an individual person but for the whole human history and for the entire cosmos.[15] Moltmann reminds us of Paul's tremendous proclamation: "So whoever is in Christ is a new creation: the old things have passed away; behold, new things have come" (2 Corinthians 5:17). Because the creative Word of God enfleshed is now actively dwelling among us, century after century, the world is being created anew in spite of and beyond the powers of destruction and death.

In these early years of the third millennium of Christian history, we need ever stronger faith in this Word made flesh and dwelling among us. Only this Word can enable us to

talk compassionately with all peoples in ways that will manifest the beauty and wonder of the new creation, truly at work
in our world.[16] This Word made flesh is continually creating the world anew because He is "full of grace and truth"
and "from his fullness we have all received, grace in place of
grace" (John 1:14, 16).

Lamb of God

Immediately following the description of Jesus as the Word
made flesh, John's Gospel introduces Jesus as the Lamb of
God. The priests and Levites asked a different John—John
the Baptist—if he is the Messiah, or Elijah, or the Prophet,
and he answered that he was not (1:21). He referred to someone who would come after him, someone whose sandal strap
John was not worthy to untie. The next day, when Jesus
walked toward him, John said, "Behold, the Lamb of God,
who takes away the sin of the world" and identified Jesus as
the one he had referred to earlier (1:29–30). The day after
that, when John was with two of his disciples, Jesus walked
by, and John said the same thing again, this time to his disciples, "Behold, the Lamb of God" (1:36).

The symbol of the lamb was quite familiar to John the
Baptist and his disciples. The Exodus story highlighted the
blood of a lamb. That first Passover celebration centered on
a lamb "slaughtered during the evening twilight" (Exodus
12:6). The blood of this sacrificial lamb was then applied
to the doorposts of the Hebrews' houses as a sign preserving
each family from God's destructive blow against the Egyptian

taskmasters (12:13). Considering the basic significance of the Exodus in the history of the Jewish people, it is not surprising that lambs continued to play a major role in their sacrificial worship.

John the Baptist's first identification of Jesus not only singles him out as the Lamb of God but also attributes to Jesus taking away the sin of the world (John 1:29). "The sin of the world" refers to the universal condition of separation and alienation from God. Taking away the sin of the world is one more way of clarifying the new creation begun by the Word made flesh and dwelling among us.

This lamb imagery also appears in the prophet-servant passages of Isaiah, but toward the end, in the fourth and final of the Servant Songs, often called the Song of the Suffering Servant (Isaiah 52:13—53:12):

> Though he was harshly treated, he submitted
> and opened not his mouth;
> Like a lamb led to the slaughter
> or a sheep before the shearers,
> he was silent and opened not his mouth.
> —Isaiah 53:7

John's Gospel relates this lamb imagery and symbolism to his portrayal of Jesus' cruel suffering and death by highlighting Jesus' pierced side from which blood and water flowed out (John 19:34). In this descriptive scene on Calvary, Jesus is seen as the sacrificial lamb who takes away—absolutely and for all time—the sin of the world.

Basic to this proclamation of Jesus as the pierced Lamb of God is our understanding of a sacrificial gift given to God whose gracious acceptance then transforms the gift. The blood of the sacrificial lamb of Exodus played a necessary role in the liberation of God's people from conditions of slavery. The blood of Jesus, the sacrificial lamb on Calvary, liberates us from sin itself—and sin's ultimate result, death—and transforms us to risen life.

We can't fully appreciate the significance of the Hebrews' Exodus from slavery in Egypt unless we understand the covenant ritual described in the book of Exodus. The twenty-fourth chapter begins by highlighting Moses' prayerfulness. "Moses alone is to come close to the Lord" (Exodus 24:2). After prayerfully communing with God, Moses prepared an altar for a sacrificial ritual that would signify the sharing of God's life with the Hebrew people. After young bulls were sacrificed as peace offerings, "Moses took half of the blood and put it in large bowls; the other half he splashed on the altar." When the people agreed to the life directives in the book of the covenant, Moses "took the blood and sprinkled it on the people" (24:6, 8).

This ritual had profound meaning for these newly covenanted people. For them, the altar symbolized God's special presence. When Moses sprinkled blood on the altar and then sprinkled blood on the people, they understood that it was the beginning of their sharing in God's life.

Lamb imagery is prominent throughout the Book of Revelation, a book attributed to John. In all the imagery describing horrendous suffering and struggle in the world, the lamb symbol speaks of hope for the ultimate triumph of God's loving power. The final chapters of this symbolic book continue to identify Jesus as Lamb of the New Jerusalem, the one who has taken away all the sin of the world. In the new heavens and new earth, God will always be with God's people.

> He will wipe every tear from their eyes, and there shall
> be no more death or mourning, wailing or pain, [for]
> the old order has passed away.—Revelation 21:4

Revelation's theology of the new creation as new heavens and new earth identifies the Lamb with the new light, a light doing away with the need for even sun or moon (Revelation 21:23). This identification of the Lamb with the new light reminds us how John's Gospel identified Jesus as the "light of the world" (John 8:12; 9:5). The Gospel had proclaimed that in the new creative process "The true light, which enlightens everyone, was coming into the world" (John 1:9). This light was truly God's Word enfleshed, the Word who becomes the Lamb of God.

Perhaps one of the main reasons the Lamb is identified with the light of the new creation was the new understanding regarding human suffering. From the Genesis account of the first creation and from the Church's developing doctrine on the origin of sin, we know that suffering came into God's good creation because of sin.[17] In proclaiming Jesus as the Lamb of God who takes away the sin of the world, we are professing our faith in the compassion of God who loves us so much that this Creator God, this Word made flesh, enters into our suffering even to the extent of suffering a cruel death.

The mystery of God's real experience of our human suffering took on more meaning for me when I recalled an early childhood experience. My baby brother was very sick, so much so that our family doctor was coming to our home. As my mother agonized over this little child crying out in pain, she exclaimed, "If only I could take that suffering to myself!" In some way, her heart was suffering as much as, if not more than, her tiny infant son. My compassionate mother, truly suffering with her child, helped me begin to understand God's compassionate love, God's true suffering with and for us.

Recently, and largely under the influence of Jürgen Moltmann, we have begun to refer to our "crucified God."[18] Latin American liberation theologian Sobrino continues to remind us of "crucified peoples." Using the phrases "crucified God" and "crucified peoples" can help us realize that our infinitely loving God truly suffers with us, and in that unity between God and us, suffering is transformed into new life. Jesus' crucifixion and death can never be separated from his entry into risen life.

One of the most powerful reminders of the significance of Jesus' name Lamb of God is the broken statue displayed at the United Nations in New York. This broken statue is from an exhibit on the effects of nuclear war. This larger-than-life statue of St. Agnes was recovered from the ruins of the Urukami Cathedral in Nagasaki. St. Agnes is holding the traditional lamb. Very significantly, St. Agnes and the lamb are charred and pockmarked by atomic fire. Facing this tragic remnant of nuclear bombing, we are moved to pray, "Lamb of God, who takes away the sin of the world, grant us peace."[19]

In our celebration of the Eucharist, often referred to as the memorial of Jesus' passion, three times we refer to Jesus as the Lamb of God who takes away the sin of the world. In the Gloria we pray, "Lord Jesus Christ, only Son of the Father, Lord God, Lamb of God, you take away the sin of the world: have mercy on us." At the breaking of the bread we pray, "Lamb of God, you take away the sins of the world, have mercy on us: grant us peace." At Communion we pray, "This is the Lamb of God who takes away the sins of the world. Happy are those who are called to his supper."

How beautiful it is that this Lamb of God comes to us in every Eucharist as food, food that nourishes our compassionate love for God and all of God's family, particularly those who are suffering in any way. Perhaps one of the most pertinent realizations for us now is that we pray to the Lamb of God for the gift of peace. In this powerful prayer of every Eucharist, we are reminded that peace continues to come to us personally and communally through the Lamb of God who is united not only with the world's suffering people but also with peacemakers struggling and suffering in so many ways to bring peace into our world. Yes, happy are those called to this banquet of the Lamb where we receive God's nourishing strength and compassionate peacemaking love.

There are other names for Jesus in Scripture. But these four names—Beloved Son, Servant, Word Made Flesh, and

Lamb of God—help us see how we share divine life through, with, and in Jesus. As our friendship with Jesus matures, we grow in our relationship with God—Jesus' Abba and ours—as we look forward to the final, eternal embrace of our tripersonal God.

Questions for Reflection

1. When you read the words God the Father said to Jesus, "You are my beloved Son, in whom I am well pleased," how does that affect the way you think of God the Father?

2. If Jesus is God's beloved son, then what can we learn from Jesus about relating to God as father?

3. When you read about the Suffering Servant in Isaiah, what emotions and thoughts are evoked in you toward Jesus?

4. How do you relate to the life of a servant? How does your surrounding culture encourage or discourage you to think in terms of serving others, even to extreme levels of personal sacrifice?

5. Try to imagine how you would relate to God if God had never been made flesh in Jesus. What does it mean to you that the Word was with God from the beginning and then came to dwell among us?

6. It is unlikely that you grew up in slavery or have had any experience with blood sacrifice. How can you identify with Jesus the Lamb of God?

7. Reflect on one of Jesus' names that has particular significance for you at this time in your life. Which names mean the most to you, and why?

8. Try to identify other Gospel names for Jesus that have special meaning in today's world.

ᚫ 3 ᚫ

Jesus' Abba and Ours

"I made known to them your name."
—John 17:26

A CCORDING TO THE GOSPELS, JESUS PRAYED TO God using the endearing title of "Abba," or Father (Matthew 11:25; John 17:1–26). When the disciples asked Jesus, "Lord, teach us to pray," Jesus responded by telling them to call God "Father" (Luke 11:1–2). Matthew proclaims that Jesus said, "Our Father" (Matthew 6:9). And in the Gospel of John, when the risen Jesus appears to Mary Magdalene, he tells her to go to the disciples and tell them, "I am going to my Father and your Father, to my God and your God" (John 20:17).

Christians today face many complications when we refer to God as Father. A growing awareness of centuries-old patriarchal cultural injustices against women has resulted in great hesitancy on the part of many people to apply to God the name of Father. In the prayer life of the Church today we need great sensitivity and wisdom to cope with this situation.[1]

Today's growing emphasis on enculturation can be very helpful here. Our ready access to people of other cultures through immigration, travel, and almost instant worldwide communication through the Internet is giving us an awareness of other cultures that is unprecedented in human history. We are learning both positive and negative factors in all cultures, including our own.

In recent years, theological training has paid more attention to the human aspects of Jesus' life. We are beginning to better understand how Jesus was influenced by his own culture. For instance, we know that the Jewish religious worldview of Jesus' time had an impact on how he carried out his mission.

When Jesus prayed to God as Father, we understand that for quite some time the Jewish people had referred to God as "King-father." Rabbis had begun this prayerful practice to offset the harsh and even cruel imagery often attached to the title of "king." Israel's tragic history was caused in great part by the many despotic kings whose death-dealing actions were a far cry from the covenant relationship established with Israel's God. In other words, to offset the false, devastating image of a despotic king, the word *father* was added to remind Israel of God's extraordinary covenantal love, a love that really brought forth a relationship of family. The apostle Paul strongly reminded the early Christians, "For you did not receive a spirit of slavery to fall back into fear, but you received a spirit of adoption, through which we cry, 'Abba, Father!'" (Romans 8:15).

Abba

In recent years, considerable emphasis has been placed on Jesus' prayerful reference to God as "Abba." Our scholarship has highlighted the surprising significance involved in Jesus' use of "Abba" as an endearing title for God. As we understand the implications of this term, we can more wisely approach the unfortunate and problematic connotations often related to the title of "father."

In *Consider Jesus,* Elizabeth Johnson explains that *Abba* is the Aramaic word that a little child uses when referring to his or her father. *Abba* implies a loving, trusting relationship. In commenting on Jesus' own intimate experience of this compassionate God and on Jesus' encouragement of others to trust in his Abba, Johnson gives us this summary statement:

> Jesus' *Abba* experience is the heart of the matter, the dynamism behind his preaching the reign of God and of his typical way of acting. God *Abba* was the passion of his life.[2]

In his article "The Trinitarian Structure of Discipleship," Herman Schalück reminds us of the tremendous significance in the historical fact of Jesus' revealing God as Father. Schalück provides helpful insight on the term *Abba*:

> There is one important observation that is crucial to a renewed theology of the Father in our time, i.e., when Jesus speaks about the Father, he does so very

personally and intimately. According to J. Jeremias,
the Aramaic word "abba" (cf. Gal. 4:6; Rom. 8:15)
that Jesus employs belongs to Jesus' *ipsissima vox*.
The use of Abba is characteristic of Jesus' relationship to God. It is a familiar expression that must
have been scandalous to Judaism.[3]

We need to remember the significance of Abba, even though
the original Aramaic of Jesus' day is still sometimes translated to the English "father." Jesus' Abba was not a harsh,
domineering, patriarchal potentate.[4] Rather, Jesus' Abba was
the life-giving, compassionate God to whom Jesus turned
continually in prayer. In the Gospel texts that give us some
awareness of Jesus' prayer life, we can discover the beauty
and strength of Jesus' relationship with God, his Abba.

    The Passion account of Mark tells us explicitly that Jesus
prayed to Abba during the most desperate and cruel suffering
of his life (14:36). In *Christology at the Crossroads*, Sobrino
considers this prayer of Jesus in the Garden to be one of
extraordinary confidence, highlighting Jesus' complete trust
and "bearing witness to the essential relationality of Jesus'
person and life. . . . [We] hear the word 'Abba', the word that
Jesus addressed to the Father with unusual confidence."[5]

    In the chapter "The Death of Jesus" Sobrino empha-
sizes a "new realization of Jesus' cross," a realization that has
profound meaning for us as we share in the life of God the
Father, Son, and Holy Spirit.

On the cross of Jesus God himself is crucified. The
Father suffers the death of the Son and takes upon

himself all the pain and suffering of history. In this ultimate solidarity with humanity he reveals himself as the God of love, who opens up a hope and a future through the most negative side of history. Thus Christian existence is nothing less but a process of participating in this same process whereby God loves the world and hence in the very life of God.[6]

In concluding this section, Sobrino quotes Moltmann's *The Crucified God.*

The content of the doctrine of the Trinity is the real cross of Christ himself. The form of the crucified Christ is the Trinity. . . . All human history, however much it may be determined by guilt and death, is taken up into this "history of God," i.e., into the Trinity, and integrated into the future of the "history of God."[7]

Could it be possible that God has entered human history and participated in our own suffering? We must recognize that, through Jesus, this is exactly what has happened. Thus we can prayerfully contemplate God's fatherly compassion toward us—compassion that led to a tortuous death—and we can begin to understand how powerfully we are connected to God through real relationship.

When we consider God's participation in human suffering, we see clearly the compassionate nature of God. Most basically, compassion refers to a genuine sharing in the pain and suffering of another. Compassion means a certain suffering-with that grows out of heartfelt concern. How significant that the Hebrew word for a mother's womb is related to the word for compassion. Michael Downey emphasizes, "To speak of the compassion of God is to speak of God's quivering womb—a womb that trembles at the sight of the frailty, suffering, and weakness of the child."[8] Jesus' motherly image for God comes to mind as he agonized compassionately over Jerusalem.

> "Jerusalem, Jerusalem, you who kill the prophets and stone those sent to you, how many times I yearned to gather your children together, as a hen gathers her young under her wings, but you were unwilling!"—Matthew 23:37

If Jesus would have waited until the beginning of this millennium to become one of us, perhaps his name for God would have been different. Jesus knew far better than we ever could that no name could express fully God's love for us.

But in whatever ways today's Christians refer to God in prayer, we can continue to be informed by Jesus' term of *Abba* to represent God's posture toward us. Let us not, through our quibbling over names, titles, and translations, inadvertently jeopardize our growing awareness of God's desire to be in intimate relationship with us. In new ways may Jesus' own prayer to his Abba be fulfilled. "Holy Father, keep them in your name that you have given me, so that they may be one just as we are" (John 17:11).

The Father's Kingdom

In both Matthew's and Luke's Gospels, Jesus teaches the disciples to pray for the coming of our Father's kingdom, that wondrous reign of God's love in all the circumstances of life (Matthew 6:10 and Luke 11:2).[9] To pray that the reign of God will come suggests that the reign of God is not yet here in its fullness. Praying for the coming of our Father's kingdom, that reign of universal love, calls for tremendous hope for a different future. This prayer calls also for unbounded trust in our Father's powerful love.

Immediately after this hope-filled prayer for the coming of the kingdom, a prayer for immediate needs follows. "Give us each day our daily bread" (Luke 11:3 and Matthew 6:11). Somehow, the coming reign of our Father includes a day-by-day fulfillment of life's basic needs. Those basic needs signified in the phrase "our daily bread" were the same in Jesus' time to the basic human needs in our time—food, clothing, and shelter. In every period of history, along with those basic needs for survival are the needs of the human heart for compassionate love in peaceful relationships. Such basic needs often call for forgiveness.

Although Matthew's and Luke's versions of the Our Father are not identical in all details, both versions highlight forgiveness in the context of human needs: "forgive us our debts, / as we forgive our debtors" (Matthew 6:12) and "forgive us our sins / for we ourselves forgive everyone in debt to us" (Luke 11:4). Very significantly, both Matthew and Luke relate our receiving forgiveness from God to our offering forgiveness to others. Both versions of this prayer that Jesus taught emphasize the need for our Father's undaunted help in the ongoing struggle against evil.

Each and every petition in this prayer is necessary for the reign of our Father's love to come about. Jesus was able to give us this profoundly simple prayer because he knew from experience what our needs are. At the beginning of his public life, Jesus announced the coming of the reign of his Abba's love:

> After John had been arrested, Jesus came to Galilee proclaiming the gospel of God: "This is the time of fulfillment. The kingdom of God is at hand. Repent, and believe in the gospel."—Mark 1:14–15

Throughout his life Jesus witnessed to the actions that would help bring about this reign—feeding the hungry, healing the sick, forgiving even his enemies, and proclaiming and explaining what the reign of God really meant.

As disciples of Jesus, we are with him on the way to the fullness of our Father's kingdom. In Jesus we discover the way of life the kingdom calls forth. Sobrino helps clarify what it means that we share in Jesus' way of bringing about the reign of God. In his *Christology at the Crossroads*, he explains:

> Jesus preaching about God is always framed in the context of his proclamation about the "Kingdom of God." Implied in that expression is a transformation of all reality—personal, social, even cosmic—

through which the reality of God will be revealed in a definitive way. The essential reality of God is inseparably bound up with the operative reality of the reign of God.[10]

As we pray the prayer that Jesus taught us, we become more and more aware that the fulfillment of the basic needs we are praying for call for some radical transformations of the societal structures that continue to enslave people in "the hellish cycle of poverty."[11] As we follow Jesus more closely on the way to our Father and to the final fulfillment of God's reign of love, we begin to know from experience that this way often brings resistance and opposition to the kingdom. We can recall Paul's warning to the early Christian community in Rome. In Romans 8:15, after reminding them of the "spirit of adoption" enabling them to call God Abba, Paul wrote, "if [we are] children, then heirs, heirs of God and joint heirs with Christ, if only we suffer with him so that we may also be glorified with him" (Romans 8:17). Paul knew that, especially in times of suffering, being with Jesus on the way to our Abba calls for undaunted trust and often for "hope against hope."[12] In his letter to the Colossians, Paul confronts us with another statement of faith in light of suffering for God's kingdom.

> Now I rejoice in my sufferings for your sake, and in my flesh I am filling up what is lacking in the afflictions of Christ on behalf of his body, which is the church.—Colossians 1:24

Paul is convinced that he is continuing Jesus' way of bringing about the reign of Abba. Paul knew by experience that this way meant suffering. Paul also knew that as with Christians of all times, this intimate sharing in Jesus' way leads to the final embrace of our Father in the ultimate completion of God's reign of compassionate love.

Jesus' Compassionate Abba

One day as I was working on this text, I noticed outside the window a flock of sparrows that was enjoying some nourishing food from the grass next to Loyola's library. How readily Luke's Gospel came to mind. "How much more important are you than birds! . . . do not worry anymore. . . . your Father knows [what you need]" (12:24, 29–30). This Gospel had already highlighted the human need for daily bread in its presentation of the prayer that Jesus taught his disciples (11:2–4). Here, this consideration of a few ravens reminds the disciples once again of their Father's continual life-giving care.

How persistently Luke's Gospel highlights forgiveness as one of the most needed blessings in the human family. Probably the most familiar parable from the Gospel of Luke is that of the lost, or prodigal, son (15:11–32). Even though the parable's title focuses on the son, the parable highlights the compassionate, forgiving father. What a joyful, celebrative climax—a lavish party testifying to the father's wholehearted forgiveness!

In Luke's account of Jesus' Sermon on the Plain, Jesus' finishes his most challenging and "scandalous teaching" on forgiving our enemies with the command, "Be merciful, just as [also] your Father is merciful" (6:36). Matthew's similar text from his Sermon on the Mount is usually translated "So be perfect, just as your heavenly Father is perfect" (5:48).[13] Both Matthew and Luke put these invitational commands in their accounts of Jesus' prophetic teachings on love and forgiveness toward enemies. Luke stresses compassion—a suffering-with experiential understanding of another's pain—as necessary in the process of genuine forgiveness. Matthew emphasizes the necessity of God's action in making us whole, in making us "perfect" as our compassionate heavenly Father.

Relating these two Gospel texts gives us particular understanding regarding Jesus' hope for us who share his life as children of God. We are to be formed as compassionate people, witnessing in unmistakable ways Abba's compassionate love.

In the Gospel of John, Jesus gave the commandment "Love one another as I love you" and added to this: "I have called you friends, because I have told you everything I have heard from my Father" (15:12, 15). One of the most important actions Jesus learned from his Father was the offering of love and forgiveness to those who had hurt him, to those who would be considered enemies rather than friends.

Being hurt always calls for a response of some sort. The hurt may be slight or grave. The hurt may be between persons, between communities, or between nations. The hurting situation is a crisis situation, small or grievous, calling for a decision of response. Whether the parties involved know it or not, a response of forgiveness can be made only under the influence of the Befriending Spirit.

In recent years, some persons actively involved in peace-making efforts have developed a process of "compassionate listening."[14] The process calls for heartfelt listening to the pain and suffering in a perceived enemy's life. This compassionate listening is a necessary prelude to authentic forgiveness. The process develops a suffering-with understanding that can culminate in genuine forgiveness and love of formerly perceived enemies. In unforeseen ways, the process of compassionate listening transforms a broken relationship into a new understanding love, a wholeness, a "perfection" that is truly a sharing in the compassionate love of Jesus' Abba.

John Paul II's Message for World Peace Day, January 1, 2002, emphasized the absolute necessity of compassionate forgiveness in today's world, so filled with violent killing:

> No peace without justice, no justice without forgiveness: that is what I wish to say to believers and unbelievers alike, to all men and women of good will who are concerned for the good of the human family and for its future.[15]

Jesus' Prayer to Our Father

Both Matthew and Luke give us insight into Jesus' prayer in which he addresses God as Father, his Abba. The texts are almost identical; however, Luke begins by highlighting Jesus' joy in the Holy Spirit:

At that very moment he rejoiced [in] the holy Spirit
and said, "I give you praise, Father, Lord of heaven and
earth, for although you have hidden these things from
the wise and the learned you have revealed them to the
childlike. Yes, Father, such has been your gracious will.
All things have been handed over to me by my Father.
No one knows who the Son is except the Father, and
who the Father is except the Son and anyone to whom
the Son wishes to reveal him."—Luke 10:21–22

How significant that Luke begins this text with reference
to the Holy Spirit! Luke reminds us that the Befriending
Spirit's influence is crucial to Jesus' life of prayer as well as to
ours. It is the same Holy Spirit who enables us to know God
in a loving relationship similar to the one Jesus experienced.
Both Matthew and Luke emphasize Jesus' desire to reveal
this loving relationship to those who can be considered
God's children.

From these texts we can see what is so basic to the life
of faith. A meaningful prayer life depends primarily on the
image of God that prevails in a person's consciousness. False
god images, such as a relentlessly punishing god or a warrior
god, cripple the life of prayer. In all honesty, we really cannot respond in a loving way to such a false god. This crippled
relationship with God also influences people's attitudes
about themselves and their relationships with others.[16]

Jesus was quite aware of what a fundamental influence
an image of God had on a person's life. His Jewish heritage

was emphatically clear—God loved them compassionately, as they knew from experience, beginning with the exodus from Egypt. In establishing the covenant between God and the people, Moses proclaimed the absolute necessity of rejecting false gods. Every aspect of life as God's *covenanted* people depended on their being faithful to their compassionate God, who had liberated them from slavery.

The relationship between God and the people of Israel is summarized in Deuteronomy 6:4–5:

> "Hear, O Israel! The LORD is our God, the LORD alone! Therefore, you shall love the LORD, your God, with all your heart, and with all your soul, and with all your strength."

Jesus clarified the relationship between this basic love of God and love of one's neighbor. When answering a lawyer's question about inheriting eternal life, Jesus added a most important statement to the familiar text from Deuteronomy:

> "Your shall love the Lord, your God, with all your heart, with all your being, with all your strength, and with all your mind, and your neighbor as yourself."—Luke 10:27

At the Last Supper, Jesus culminated this teaching with his new commandment "This is my commandment: love one another as I love you" (John 15:12). This Gospel's author presents this new commandment of love in the prayerful setting of the Eucharist.

Important Clues from the Last Supper

John's Gospel provides even more insight into the relationship between Jesus and his Abba-God. Repeatedly, Jesus refers to the oneness he enjoys with God his Father. One of the most emphatic statements of Jesus regarding this union is in the parable of the Good Shepherd. Jesus concludes his explanation of the shepherd by simply stating, "The Father and I are one" (John 10:30).

This statement of Jesus' oneness with his Father is basic to the passage in John that recounts Jesus' Last Supper with his disciples, when he reveals the new covenant of his body and blood. This is the last time he will be able to talk freely with his disciples until after his resurrection. The topics of this conversation are the most crucial in Jesus' mind, and one he keeps returning to is his desire to share with his friends the union he already has with his heavenly Father.

This teaching on the oneness Jesus enjoys with his Abba is sounded throughout the lengthy passage in John 14–17 known as the Eucharistic Discourse. In response to Thomas's question about where Jesus was going, Jesus identifies himself as "the way and the truth and the life." Jesus also clarifies where the way leads: "No one comes to the Father except through me. If you know me, then you will also know my Father. From now on you do know him and have seen him" (14:6–7).

When Philip responds to this by asking Jesus to show the Father to his disciples, Jesus proclaims, "Whoever has seen me has seen the Father" (John 14:9). Then Jesus raises a crucial question: "Do you not believe that I am in the Father and the Father is in me?" (John 14:10). How strongly Jesus emphasizes the necessity of faith in this oneness he enjoys with his Abba, a unity evident in all his words and works:

> The words that I speak to you I do not speak on my own. The Father who dwells in me is doing his works. Believe me that I am in the Father and the Father is in me, or else, believe because of the works themselves.—John 14:10–11

Jesus promises a real sharing of life with those who respond to him in faith: "Amen, amen, I say to you, whoever believes in me will do the works that I do, and will do greater ones than these, because I am going to the Father" (John 14:12). Jesus answers another disciple's question by promising a special presence with those who are faithful to him. "Whoever loves me will keep my word, and my Father will love him, and we will come to him and make our dwelling with him" (14:23).

After promising this special presence of himself and his Abba, Jesus then speaks of the coming Advocate, the comforting Holy Spirit:

> I have told you this while I am with you. The Advocate, the holy Spirit that the Father will send in

my name—he will teach you everything and remind
you of all that [I] told you.—John 14:25–26

Jesus had already identified this Advocate as "the Spirit
of truth," whom his disciples could recognize because of
the Spirit's abiding presence dwelling within them (John
14:16–17). Later Jesus highlighted once again the coming of
this "Spirit of truth that proceeds from the Father" (15:26).

During this important discourse—a climax of all the
discussions he's had with his disciples—Jesus gives us explicit
references to a tripersonal God. In the space of a few verses,
he explains that he and the Father will both dwell within the
believer and that the Holy Spirit will soon come to help the
disciples in their life of faith. As he continues, Jesus presents
the teaching of the vine and its branches as an image of our
relationship to him, the intimate sharing of his life with us.
"I have called you friends, because I have told you everything
I have heard from my Father" (John 15:15).

I am the true vine, and my Father is the vine grower.
He takes away every branch in me that does not bear
fruit, and every one that does he prunes so that it
bears more fruit. You are already pruned because of
the word that I spoke to you. Remain in me, as I
remain in you. Just as a branch cannot bear fruit on
its own unless it remains in the vine, so neither can
you unless you remain in me. I am the vine, you are
the branches. Whoever remains in me and I in him

will bear much fruit, because without me you can do
nothing.—John 15:1–5

Jesus makes it clear that we are called to live on in his
love because he loves us as the Father has loved him (John
15:9–10). The reason for this beautiful love is nothing less
than joy: "I have told you this so that my joy may be in you
and your joy may be complete" (John 15:11).

From experience Jesus knew his disciples would suffer
rejection and persecution. Once again he promises that the
Spirit of truth will be with his own to continually guide
them in the truth of his Father's love for them and that in
this love they will find peace (John 16:13, 33).

In John 17:13, as Jesus turns directly to his Abba in prayer,
he prays that all of his disciples may share his joy completely.
He begins the prayer by requesting that the Father's glory
be shared with Jesus and his friends (17:1–5, 10). Jesus prays
that his disciples will be made holy by the truth of his Abba's
love for them (17:17–19). And he is praying not only for
the disciples who are with him at that moment, but also all
"those who will believe in me through their word" (17:20).
Jesus prays "that they may all be one, as you, Father, are in
me and I in you" (17:21).

The prayer concludes with Jesus' promise to continue
revealing the name of his Abba so that his disciples will truly
share the life of love that Jesus knows. "I made known to
them your name and I will make it known, that the love
with which you loved me may be in them and I in them"
(John 17:26).

This prayer of Jesus is one of the most treasured sections of the New Testament. How clearly he prays that his followers will share his life of love, the life of compassionate love he shares with his Abba in the oneness of the Holy Spirit. Everything depends on this sharing of life.[17]

Not only does Jesus pray that his disciples will share evermore completely in the relationship he knows with his Abba, but he also gives the gift of himself as food to nourish that life in ever stronger and more vibrant ways. In the context of Eucharistic life, this prayer begins to manifest Jesus' deepest desires to share his divine tripersonal life with us in our life now and in eternity. And Jesus is very practical. He knows we cannot enjoy this life without the continual nourishment of his body and blood; in this mysterious way we are able to participate in this life as Jesus' brothers and sisters, and as children of Abba-Father.

Questions for Reflection

1. What is the significance of Jesus' naming God "Abba"? What are some of the names/titles you might use for God as you understand God at this time in your life?

2. When you see or hear the phrase "kingdom of God," what comes to mind? What would the fulfilled kingdom of God look like? How do we, as brothers and sisters of Jesus and as children of Abba, participate in bringing this kingdom to fulfillment?

3. In response to the prayer that Jesus taught us, how might people become more involved in providing for people's daily needs?

4. Reflect on your experience of giving and receiving forgiveness. What made such forgiveness possible? What experience have you had with compassionate listening?

5. How does your relationship with Jesus help you love your neighbor? As you reflect upon your loving human relationships, try to identify how those relationships have been influenced by your awareness of Abba's love and of the help of Befriending Spirit.

6. What does it mean to "be one" with someone, outside of sexual intimacy? When Jesus talked about being one with the Father, what do you think he was trying to convey? And what does that mean to you in daily life?

4

The Meaning of God as Tripersonal

"Remain in me, as I remain in you."
—John 15:4

JESUS MAKES AN AMAZING STATEMENT IN THE Gospel of John when he talks about himself as the Good Shepherd: "I came so that they might have life and have it more abundantly" (John 10:10). He goes on to say, "I am the good shepherd, and I know mine and mine know me, just as the Father knows me and I know the Father; and I will lay down my life for the sheep" (John 10:14–15). In this proclamation, Jesus promises to truly share his life with us, just as the Father shares life with Jesus.

Jesus continues to clarify the meaning of this life that he shares with his Abba and the Holy Spirit. In the Gospel of John chapter 15, Jesus uses the image of a vine and its branches to help us grasp the reality of sharing life with him, with the Father, and with the Holy Spirit. Jesus promises complete joy because of this gift of friendship (John 15:11).

This gift is made possible by the Befriending Spirit, and it gives glory to God the Father (John 15:8).

Through Jesus' use of these images—the vine and the shepherd—his earliest disciples began to understand how intimately connected Jesus was to his Abba, the heavenly Father and the Holy Spirit. These early Christians began to realize that Jesus was revealing to them a divine tripersonal life and that this tripersonal experience of God aligned with the God they already understood. The God of Israel, the compassionate One had freed them from Egyptian bondage and had brought them through the wilderness and into the Promised Land. As Jesus lived among his disciples and loved them, he introduced to them an expanded view of this God of the Jewish people and their exodus. The life Jesus shared with his disciples was the same as the life—and love—the Father and Holy Spirit shared with him.

The Right Language

Finding suitable and meaningful language to express the wonder of God's loving, active presence in their lives always had been a challenge in Israel's history. How those first Christians of Jewish upbringing must have cherished Jesus' words and images that gave some meaning to the divine life he was beginning to share with them.

Although the earliest Christians lived under Roman domination, the influence of Greek culture was predominant in many ways. As the Good News spread into the Greek world, the early Christians had to learn how to translate effectively a concept of the loving, relational God Jesus had revealed to them.[1]

The Greeks were quite advanced in philosophy—that is, human wisdom concerned with the created universe. Living in that culture, Christians developed new vocabulary patterns to clarify the basic truths of faith revealed in and by Jesus. They began to express gospel truths with new words, such as *Incarnation* and *Trinity*.

Philosophical understandings of *person* and *nature* began to play an important role as Christians attempted to harmonize Jesus' teachings with the human wisdom of Greek culture. Those early clarifications of *person* and *nature* have provided basic insight into God's being and are familiar to Christians today. We refer to God as three Persons in one divine nature. We believe Jesus has two natures in one person. We know that these mysteries of our faith are beyond comprehension, but we can always discover more about the wonder and beauty of our God as revealed in Jesus.

From our human experience we understand that "person" refers to *who one is* and that "nature" refers to *what a being does*. Such philosophical distinctions came about through reflection on the created universe. When such philosophical clarifications are applied to God, however, we must realize the limitations of such language.

Person and nature language applied to God uses *philosophical analogy*, which is a way in which we apply human understanding to divine reality. Analogy indicates both likeness and difference. There is both similarity and difference between person and nature in God and person and nature in human beings. Creatures are not God. Although human persons, male and female, are created in the image and likeness of God (Genesis 1:27), the mystery of God cannot be expressed totally in any creature, nor described comprehensively in human language.[2]

However, through the centuries and in various cultures, people who have known and enjoyed a prayerful union with God have articulated profound insight into the mystery of God. In Christian faith, *person* and *nature* have been helpful concepts for expressing God's love as revealed in the life of Jesus. Usually Christians can articulate their faith in Jesus as human and divine, even if they have little or no understanding of how Jesus' human and divine natures existed together in one Person. Most Christians can articulate their faith in one God in three divine Persons. We have often referred to God's "threeness in oneness," using for illustration the well-known shamrock plant with its threefold leaves on one stem, an image for the Trinity attributed to Saint Patrick. However, one of the limitations of this imagery is that a plant is impersonal.

It is not surprising that the philosophical concept of relationship was prominent in the early teaching about the Trinity—God's tripersonal nature. When we use the word *person*, that language calls forth the remembrance of relationships we have experienced. We understand how significant relationships are, whether their impact is negative or positive. And so Jesus' use of personal language in describing the relationships between him, Abba, and Holy Spirit make the concept of God more understandable to us. Philosophical understandings can be quite helpful, but Jesus' own experience will always be the basic foundation for our faith in God as three in one.

Two other philosophical terms, *immanent* and *economic*, refer to how we share in God's three-in-one nature. Especially today, those Trinitarian references can be quite confusing, particularly the word *economic*, a term we use most frequently in the context of finances. But these two words have been used to distinguish divine life within God (*immanent*) and divine life that God actively shares with us in the world (*economic*).

Theologian Karl Rahner insists that the economic Trinity is also the immanent Trinity.[3] Here and now in this world, we genuinely share in God's life (economic). The life God shares with us is the same life existing within the relationship among the Father, the Son, and the Holy Spirit (immanent).

Why We Say "Tripersonal"

In recent years the word *tripersonal* has been used more frequently along with the words *triune* and *Trinitarian*.[4] This shift in language has been influenced by renewed interest in the Bible, particularly within the ranks of the Catholic Church, since Vatican II. We have become much more familiar with Jesus' way of referring to God as indicated in the Gospels and with the earliest Christians' understandings as indicated in the Epistles. Referring to God as tripersonal immediately focuses on the mystery of three divine Persons, whose life is a communion of loving relationships. This is the divine tripersonal life that Jesus proclaimed and that he wants to share with us.

We understand that each human person is not quite like any other. This personal uniqueness is also true of divine Persons in some analogous way. Although the Father, the Son, and the Holy Spirit do exist in unity, each is unique from the others. Jesus refers to the Father's actions in ways that are somewhat different from the actions of the Holy Spirit. Jesus himself is set apart in some ways from the Father and the Holy Spirit.

One way we can grow in appreciation of the unique Persons of the Trinity is to ponder their names and actions as we know them from Scripture. We have already considered the actions of the Holy Spirit that have resulted in the special name Befriending Spirit. The initiating role of God's Spirit is necessary for human participation, through friendship, in the divine life. The Befriending Spirit is given to us as a gift—a gift we must receive freely. Then God's befriending Spirit initiates a new creation with new communities who participate in friendship with God and with one another. This life of friendship depends on a maturing prayerfulness as indicated so clearly in the community of believers (Acts 1:14).

We have not only the name of the human person Jesus, but we also have designations that help us understand Jesus' uniqueness: Beloved Son, Servant, Word Made Flesh, and Lamb of God. Each name enables us to see some aspect of his unique relation to his Abba, to the Spirit, and to us. In Jesus we see how divine life is lived humanly.

The purpose of Jesus' entire ministry was to bring about the reign of Abba, whose compassionate love would make all the difference in the world. Especially in Jesus' life of prayer do we see some indications of the beautiful relationship Jesus enjoyed with his Abba. Particularly in the Eucharistic Discourse, culminating in Jesus' prayer, we discover the beauty of that relationship.

And what is almost beyond belief is Jesus' heartfelt desire to share this life of love with us: "I made known to them your name and I will make it known, that the love with which you loved me may be in them and I in them" (John 17:26).

More Abundant Life

In John's Gospel, Jesus said, "I came so that they might have life and have it more abundantly" (John 10:10). In Paul's letter to the Galatians, Paul insisted, "no longer I, but Christ lives in me" (Galatians 2:20). This life that Jesus promises and bestows on us is in reality our participation in the divine life he lived humanly as he walked the earth. We recognize that life of love through Jesus' actions. We grow in our understanding of that life through Jesus' teachings. We cherish that life more and more in our prayerful union with him.

Every Eucharistic Prayer culminates in the phrase "through him, with him and in him, in the unity of the Holy Spirit, all glory and honor is yours, almighty Father, for ever and ever." What do these terms—*through, with,* and *in*—really mean in our relationship with Jesus?[5]

The preposition *through* indicates some kind of movement, a "going somewhere" from one place or situation to another. At the Last Supper, Thomas asked Jesus a key question: "Master, we do not know where you are going; how can we know the way?" Jesus said to him, "I am the way and the truth and the life. No one comes to the Father except *through* me" (John 14:5–6, italics added).

Here Jesus clarifies that only through him can anyone come to God the Father—his Abba and ours. Jesus truly is the way, continually witnessing to the compassionate love he shares with Abba and the Befriending Spirit. The more we experience this way in our following of Jesus, the more we realize we are truly with him and in him.[6]

The preposition *with* denotes a relation of oneness, of union. This oneness with Jesus on the way to his Abba can happen only through the action of the Befriending Spirit, who continually strengthens and beautifies the friendship Jesus proclaimed when he said, "I have called you friends, because I have told you everything I have heard from my Father" (John 15:15).

Jesus had already spoken of the oneness his friends would enjoy. "Whoever loves me will keep my word, and my Father will love him, and we will come to him and make our dwelling *with* him" (John 14:23, italics added).

The image of the dwelling place speaks to the preposition *in*, which is one more way to express an intimate union, a oneness even beyond the concepts of *through* and *with*. In promising the gift of himself in the Eucharist,

Jesus spoke of this intimate union: "Whoever eats my flesh and drinks my blood remains *in* me and I *in* him" (John 6:56, italics added).

How clearly the first letter of John describes the wondrous effects of God's dwelling in us:

> No one has ever seen God. Yet, if we love one another, God remains in us, and his love is brought to perfection in us. . . . God is love, and whoever remains in love remains in God and God in him.
> —1 John 4:12, 16

In Jesus we really begin to experience the more abundant life he promised. And Jesus understood that our sharing in the love relationship he knew with his Abba and the Holy Spirit enables us to know the joy he himself knew. "I have told you this so that my joy may be in you and your joy may be complete" (John 15:11).

Through, with, and in Jesus Today

As we enjoy divine life through, with, and in Jesus, we learn more and more how important all of our relationships are, not only with God but with one another in the human family and with the whole of creation. We also begin to understand the significance of mutuality, a sharing of life that is free from domination in its many forms. Today's feminist theologians emphasize continually the necessity of appreciating and developing mutual loving relationships in all aspects of living.

In *She Who Is,* Elizabeth Johnson entitled a chapter "Women's Interpreted Experience." In it she writes:

> The particular pattern of relationship consistently promoted in feminine ethical discourse is mutuality. This signifies a relation marked by equivalence between persons, a concomitant valuing of each other, a common regard marked by trust, respect, and affection in contrast to competition, domination, or assertions of superiority. It is a relationship on the analogy of friendship, an experience often used as metaphor to characterize the reciprocity/independence dialectic at the heart of all caring relationships.[7]

This greatly needed emphasis on mutuality resonates with Jesus' actions and teachings. For instance, his imagery of the vine and the branches makes obvious the mutual flowing of life from one to the other. The vine cannot exist without the branches. The branches cannot exist without the vine. Their mutual sharing of life brings forth abundant fruit (John 15:1–8).

In his first letter to the Corinthians, Paul used the image of the Body of Christ to describe our mutual sharing in the life of Jesus. "As a body is one though it has many parts, and all the parts of the body, though many, are one body, so also Christ" (1 Corinthians 12:12).

In our times, the second chapter of Vatican II's *Dogmatic Constitution on the Church, Lumen Gentium* (Light to All

Nations), proclaims our mutual sharing of divine life when we are called the people of God:

> It has pleased God, however, to make [us] holy and save [us] not merely as individuals without any mutual bonds, but by making them into a single people, a people which acknowledges Him in truth and serves Him in holiness. (LG 9)

This thought is taken even further in the preface of Vatican II's *Pastoral Constitution on the Church* also known as *Gaudium et Spes*.

> The joys and the hopes, the griefs and the anxieties of the people of this age, especially those who are poor or in any way afflicted, these too are the joys and hopes, the griefs and anxieties of the followers of Christ. Indeed, nothing genuinely human fails to raise an echo in their hearts. (GS 1)

This preface concludes by identifying the Befriending Spirit as leading the way for the followers of Christ to continue Jesus' work as they share his life. "Inspired by no earthly ambition, the Church seeks but a solitary goal: to carry forward the work of Christ under the lead of the befriending Spirit" (GS 3).

Subsequent chapters of this Pastoral Constitution describe people's critical needs in the areas of human dignity, family, cultural development, socioeconomic life, political community, fostering of peace, and the promotion of a community of nations.

The Risky Ways of God

We may not immediately relate the Church's social teachings to God's tripersonal life and how we share in that life. But we can always think in terms of what our personal actions say about our relationships with Jesus, God our Abba, and the Befriending Spirit. And we can recall, again and again, Jesus' emphasis on his actions as growing out of his personal relationship with God the Father: "The works that the Father gave me to accomplish, these works that I perform testify on my behalf that the Father has sent me" (John 5:36).

It's easy to become overwhelmed by the scope of social needs challenging the people of God. Today's social problems are somewhat different from those Jesus dealt with during his earthly ministry. It's not always easy to see how the urgent problems cited in the documents of Vatican II involve the abundant life Jesus promised us. But the urgency of these world problems makes it increasingly pertinent to see societal and ecological involvements in compassionate understanding and love as expressions of the mutual divine life we experience through, with, and in Jesus.

Paul Wadell's recent essay entitled "The Subversive Ethics of the Kingdom of God" is subtitled "Witnessing the frightening creativity of Jesus." Wadell writes:

> To appreciate the moral impact of Jesus' proclamation of the kingdom of God, however, we must

realize that Jesus' primary aim was not to hand on
to us a collection of moral principles, much less a
handbook for solving sticky moral dilemmas; rather
Jesus came to renew Israel by creating a people who
would embody in their everyday lives the promising,
if risky, ways of God in the world.[8]

The "promising, if risky, ways of God in the world" are often
referred to as works of justice and peacemaking. In his essay
"Biblical Perspectives on Justice," John Donahue clarified
the meaning of justice in a most basic and helpful way: "In
general terms the biblical idea of justice can be described as
fidelity to the demands of a relationship."[9] We must understand that a person's relationship to God is basic for right
relationships with other persons and with all of creation.
Loving relationships with all of God's creation really depend
on our relationship with God. Our fidelity to the demands of
this basic relationship means that we respond in faithful love
to the love God shares with us through, with, and in Jesus.
And our being faithful to the demands of justice really grows
out of our faithfulness to loving all of God's creatures.

When Jesus invited his disciples to "love one another as
I love you" (John 15:12), he was calling for justice in a most
basic way. Jesus was really clarifying the meaning of justice
for those who shared his life. True justice cannot exist or
thrive without loving relationships:

Action on behalf of justice and participation in
the transformation of the world fully appear to us

as a constitutive dimension of the preaching of the Gospel, or, in other words, of the Church's mission for the redemption of the human race and its liberation from every oppressive situation. (JW 6)

At the beginning of this new millennium, John Paul II emphasized the challenge of forgiveness in the cry for justice and peace. Forgiveness implies hurt and suffering in relationships that call for healing—healing that can happen only through compassionate love that is strong and faithful enough to restore relationship, both personal and societal. Our participation in divine life demands that, in our lives, we practice forgiveness.[10]

How prophetically John Paul II proclaimed the absolute necessity of forgiveness in his World Day of Peace Address of 2002. After reminding us of Jesus' prayer on the cross, "Father, forgive them, they know not what they do" (Luke 23:34)—a prayer expressing a personal decision to forgive—John Paul II points out that forgiveness "has a divine source and criterion" but is also a "fully human act." He continues:

Forgiveness, therefore as a fully human act, is above all a personal initiative. But individuals are essentially social beings, situated within a pattern of relationships through which they express themselves in ways both good and bad. Consequently, society, too, is absolutely in need of forgiveness.

Families, groups, societies, states and the international community itself need forgiveness in order to renew ties that have been sundered, go beyond sterile situations of mutual condemnation and overcome the temptation to discriminate against others without appeal. The ability to forgive lies at the very basis of the idea of a future society marked by justice and solidarity.[11]

As we face the daunting challenges of justice and peacemaking in the world, it becomes increasingly necessary for us to draw upon the strength of the Eucharist. During the Last Supper, Jesus explained that we must draw our spiritual sustenance from him. Also, in the sixth chapter of John, Jesus speaks of God's bread for the life of the world:

> For the bread of God is that which comes down from heaven and gives life to the world. . . . I am the living bread that came down from heaven; whoever eats this bread will live forever; and the bread that I will give is my flesh for the life of the world.
> —John 6:33, 51

Through the Eucharist, we live through Christ, with Christ, and in Christ, in the unity of the Holy Spirit. The salvation of the whole world depends upon how well we dwell in this relationship and how consistently we receive the nourishment of Jesus' body and blood.

Only as we grow closer in our relationship to our Abba, as we live in Jesus as intimately as a branch lives in a vine, and as we rely on the power and companionship of the Befriending Spirit can we truly witness to God's compassion and demonstrate divine love to the world around us.

Questions for Reflection

1. Reflect on one scriptural image that gives you some insight into God's desire to share divine life with us.

2. Make a list of statements Jesus made during his Eucharistic Discourse (John 14–17) that refer to our sharing in divine life.

3. Choose one of the statements you listed for question 2, and explore what that statement means to you personally.

4. How has the Trinity been explained to you at various times and places in your life? What descriptions have worked best in helping you understand God's presence to us as Abba, Jesus, and Befriending Spirit?

5. Explain, in your own words, what it means to live "through" Jesus, "with" Jesus, and "in" Jesus.

6. Why are loving relationships essential to the Church's social actions?

ॐ 5 ॐ

Making All Thing New

"Behold, I make all things new."
—Revelation 21:5

T HE FIRST TWO CHAPTERS OF GENESIS RECOUNT
God's graciousness in making all things good. In
the third chapter we see how humans reject God's
design—and flee from a relationship with God. While we
understand that Genesis is not a historical account, we can
attend to it seriously as a tragic literary portrayal of the
human refusal to believe in the goodness of God.[1]

Renewing the Face of the Earth

The devastating results of this human refusal to believe in
God's goodness are described in vivid imagery in Genesis
chapters 3—11. Adam and Eve no longer enjoy God's company in the garden; they hide from God, hardly an act of
friendship. Adam and Eve are no longer comfortable with
themselves; they cover their nakedness. And they begin to
know hardship and suffering. They experience the jealousy

and hatred of one son toward his brother: Cain kills Abel. The wickedness of Adam and Eve's descendants brings forth a devastating flood all over the earth: "In the eyes of God the earth was corrupt and full of lawlessness" (Genesis 6:11).

Even though God saved Noah, "a good man and blameless in that age, for he walked with God" and with Noah God saved his family and pairs of "all other living creatures" (Genesis 6:9, 10, 18–19), the Genesis story does not end with the human family's faithfulness to God's new covenant, signified by a rainbow (Genesis 9:9). The first eleven chapters end with another tragic rejection of the good and gracious creator God. The people planned to build a "tower with its top in the sky" in order to make a name for themselves (Genesis 11:4). Those plans grew out of the arrogant decision to reject God's design and to substitute it with human ego and effort. Once more, humanity rejected God and God's creative designs. As a result, the human family became divided and dispersed when God confused their language and thus stopped the tower's construction (Genesis 11:8–9).[2]

The vivid imagery of these early chapters of Genesis can become more understandable and meaningful to us if we relate it to the experience of Moses receiving God's commandments on Mount Sinai (Exodus 20). There the first commandment highlights the absolute necessity of faithfulness to the compassionate God who rescued the people from slavery. This first commandment makes clear that human response to a loving, caring God is basic to all other aspects of life.

We need to understand those first eleven chapters of Genesis in order to appreciate the Pentecost event described

in the beginning chapters of Acts. When Jesus' followers
received the Befriending Spirit, this initiated a new bonding
in the human family. In Genesis, a confusion of language
divided people; in Acts, people from many different places
heard Jesus' disciples speaking, each "in his own language"
(Acts 2:6). The tragic results of the human rejection of God
as described in Genesis were beginning to be transformed. A
whole new creation was beginning.[3]

As Luke describes this new beginning in the earliest
chapters of Acts, he uses the literary technique of summary
statements to highlight the results of the Spirit's coming. Twice
Luke describes the actions of the new community bonding:

> They devoted themselves to the teaching of the
> apostles and to the communal life, to the breaking
> of the bread and to the prayers. . . .The community
> of believers was of one heart and one mind, and no
> one claimed that any of his possessions was his own,
> but they had everything in common. With great
> power the apostles bore witness to the resurrection
> of the Lord Jesus, and great favor was accorded
> them all. There was no needy person among them,
> for those who owned property or houses would sell
> them, bring the proceeds of the sale, and put them at
> the feet of the apostles, and they were distributed to
> each according to need.—Acts 2:42; 4:32–35

In the first summary description of Christian community
life, the English expression "communal life" does not really

express all the mutuality involved in the Greek word *koinonia*, an almost untranslatable word. The sharing and interaction of life implied in *koinonia* resonates well with Jesus' image of vine and branches (John 15:1). The sharing of a common life is indispensable in this imagery. There simply is no life without a mutual sharing. Luke's description indicates the implications of this mutual sharing of life, "of one heart and one mind."

These earliest descriptions of Christian community can help us see how loving relationships of the heart and mind depend on a prayerfulness initiated by, and attuned to, the Befriending Spirit. "Breaking of bread" is an early Christian way of referring to the Eucharist. Eucharistic breaking of bread always implies the sharing of life-giving resources with those who are hungry.

In pondering the first five chapters of Acts, which give us a picture of the earliest Christian community, it is important to realize that the coming of the Befriending Spirit occurs more than once. The fourth chapter of Acts describes another Pentecost scene when Peter and John were released and returned to the community after they had been arrested for curing a crippled man in the name of Jesus. "As they prayed, the place where they were gathered shook, and they were all filled with the holy Spirit and continued to speak the word of God with boldness" (Acts 4:31).

One reason this narrative is so important is that it bears testimony to the continuous coming of the Holy Spirit in the life of the Church. The Second Vatican Council has been described as a New Pentecost. John XXIII attributed its happening to an inspiration of the Holy Spirit, who received the new title of Befriending Spirit during the Council. The Befriending Spirit continues to be the creator Spirit, truly initiating a new creation. The more we realize the implications of this new creation, the more we understand how it is related to the dynamics of the first creation account in Genesis, in which the tragic rejection of God's friendship occurred. New creation is always involved in restoring, revitalizing, and strengthening the friendship with God that is basic and necessary for the whole creative process to happen.

Scientific discoveries impress us continually with information about the age of the universe and the immense expanse of its galaxies. The wonders of creation seem to exceed the powers of our imaginations. We can hardly imagine the expanse of time and space involved in God's beautiful creative process.

This growing awareness of creation's unfathomable wonders can be a source of tremendous hope as we enter more and more into our tripersonal God's process of making all things new. In the face of indescribable sufferings in our world, including our present ecological crisis, it is a continual challenge to maintain genuine hope for a just and peace-filled world.

We can't help but be filled with hope the more we realize that *the new creation process takes time*. We do not know the precise timeline for change and newness, nor can we project a certain parallelism with the time involved in the coming-to-be of the universe. But we can be confident that our tripersonal God is with us in our efforts to make all things new.[4] Every effort to bring about the reign of God's compassionate love is never lost, and it will bear fruit. In hopeful ways, Hermann Schalück highlighted the dynamic power of God whose creative action continues through, with, and in us:

> The trinitarian God has revealed himself as relational, as the principle of dialogue, as unity in diversity and diversity in unity, and as the dynamic reality that creates newness until the end of time.[5]

Newness and Reconciliation

New creation theology was significant in the earliest Christian communities—something we know from some of Paul's letters. One of the most explicit references to the new creation is in Paul's second letter to the Corinthians:

> So whoever is in Christ is a new creation: the old things have passed away; behold, new things have come. And all this is from God, who has reconciled us to himself through Christ and given us the ministry of reconciliation, namely, God was reconciling the world to himself in Christ, not counting their trespasses against them and entrusting to us the message of reconciliation.—2 Corinthians 5:17–19

Paul identifies the new creation with the ministry of reconciliation. All the ways in which sin has alienated creation from the peace and harmony God intended is now being restored and reconciled through Christ, who continues this reconciling ministry through us who are *in* him.

In the letter to the Ephesians we read, "And he put all things beneath his feet and gave him as head over all things to the church, which is his body, the fullness of the one who fills all things in every way" (Ephesians 1:22–23). In this letter we learn that the Church, truly Christ's body and the "fullness of him," somehow is actively present in the entire universe.

The first chapter of the letter to the Colossians gives helpful insight into this Ephesians text by identifying Christ as the "firstborn of all creation" as well as the "firstborn from the dead":

> He is the image of the invisible God,
> the firstborn of all creation.
> For in him were created all things in heaven and on
> earth,
> the visible and the invisible,
> whether thrones or dominions or principalities or
> powers;
> all things were created through him and for him.
> He is before all things,
> and in him all things hold together.
> He is the head of the body, the church.
> He is the beginning, the firstborn from the dead,
> that in all things he himself might be preeminent.
> —Colossians 1:15–18

We need to understand Israel's Exodus history in order to appreciate the powerful imagery of the term *firstborn*. During their desert wanderings the generations of Hebrews did not become familiar with the challenges of an agricultural society. When the Hebrews finally reached the Promised Land they had to learn the ways and means of agricultural life, including various fertility rituals, from the people who were acquainted with farming procedures. The offering of the firstfruit was considered a necessary ritual if the rest of the crop was to mature.

In this ancient agricultural ritual, the people understood that the life force necessary for seeds to mature came down to the earth from a fertility god or goddess. This life force was contained in the first seed beginning to sprout and had to be returned to the divine being so that this life-giving power could continue to be given to all the seeds in the entire crop. The whole harvest depended on what happened to the firstfruit. Consequently, the ritual offering of the firstfruit was crucial for the sustained life of an entire people.

Firstfruit agricultural imagery underlies the firstborn imagery applied to Jesus in Colossians. As "the firstborn of all creation. / . . . He is before all things, / and in him all things hold together" (1:15, 17). All life-giving power necessary for the new creation comes from Jesus, the firstborn of all creatures. Colossians also designates Jesus as "head of the body, the church. . . . firstborn from the dead" (1:18). All the transforming power of new life after death comes from Jesus, who is truly risen:

> For in him all the fullness was pleased to dwell,
> and through him to reconcile all things for him,
> making peace by the blood of his cross
> [through him], whether those on earth or those in
> heaven.
>
> —Colossians 1:19–20

Thus, the transforming power of the new creation is a reconciling, peace-making power. As firstborn from the dead, Jesus gives new life and peace through the power of his love in suffering and dying for all of us: "he has now reconciled in his fleshly body through his death, to present you holy, without blemish, and irreproachable before him" (Colossians 1:22).

This "firstborn" imagery then speaks more directly about the rest of the family, the Church in whom the peace-making power of Jesus' love is active in the ongoing struggle to bring about the reign of God. Again let us consider Paul's profound awareness of sharing Jesus' life as a member of the Church: "Now I rejoice in my sufferings for your sake, and in my flesh I am filling up what is lacking in the afflictions of Christ on behalf of his body, which is the church" (Colossians 1:24).

This mysterious joy in suffering must be the result of the same life-giving love that sustained Jesus especially in his excruciating suffering and death. Paul knows and proclaims this mystery of "Christ in you." To share this wisdom and life, Paul works and struggles "in accord with the exercise of his power working within me" (Colossians 1:27, 29).

In the book of Revelation, the reality of new creation is expressed in the phrase "make all things new" (21:5). The difficult imagery throughout this book describing terrible struggles and sufferings precedes this hope-filled promise proclaimed in the final two chapters. The reason for this newness, this new creation, is God's special presence with God's people, described in nuptial imagery of a new Jerusalem, the holy city, coming down out of heaven (21:2). This compassionate God who is always present "will wipe every tear from their eyes, and there shall be no more death or mourning, wailing or pain, [for] the old order has passed away" (21:4).

In these chapters of the final book of the New Testament, the risen Jesus is referred to as the triumphant Lamb of God, a title discussed in detail in chapter two of this book. This Jesus, this true Lamb of God, is the one who would take away the sin of the world (John 1:29). The risen Jesus, Lamb of God is the new light of the whole world. Jesus the compassionate Lamb really entered our suffering even to the point of a most cruel death. We recall the Lamb of God in every Eucharistic celebration, as the one who brings us peace.[6]

The book of Revelation brings us to a new level of awareness concerning God's love as expressed in the life of Jesus. This love is not only compassionate but ultimately triumphant. In proclaiming a new future, the writer of Revelation gives us necessary, ongoing hope for a radically different future. This radically hopeful outlook forms the basis of Christian eschatology, from the Greek word *eschaton*, meaning "end time" or "last things." In Christian eschatology,

God's ultimate action is the culmination of God's ongoing action through all of history. From the beginning, God has acted upon and within humanity; our very history is the story of God's action in our world. And God's ultimate action—the new heaven and new earth—is simply the outcome of God's compassion, which has been active in our lives all along.

God's ongoing action and creation is always tripersonal: now with the risen Jesus, Beloved Son, firstborn of the new creation, firstborn from the dead, in risen life at one with his Abba, continuing to send the compassionate Befriending Spirit to the Church, in order to renew the world.

Crucifixion and Hope

In his first letter to Timothy, Paul begins by referring to "Christ Jesus our hope" (1:1). The virtue of hope always looks to the future, to a time or event when present situations will be better, when present difficulties will be resolved, when needed expectations will be fulfilled. Situations of suffering can lead to hope or to despair. But in such situations, particularly those threatening death, Christ does become hope for Christians, not only in Paul's time, but throughout the centuries.

The earliest Christians knew from experience the persecution and sometimes martyrdom that resulted from following Jesus. Like Paul, those first Christians knew that somehow they were beginning to fill up "what is lacking in the afflictions of Christ" (Colossians 1:24). They were continuing and completing Christ's sufferings. Then and now, faith-filled Christians know that suffering will lead to risen life, to a new heaven and a new earth. Faith-filled Christians also know that the new heaven and new earth will not come to be unless we participate in the sufferings of Jesus Christ crucified.

The mystery of human suffering continues to raise critical questions about the goodness of God. Unfortunately, and often through false teaching and mistaken ideas, suffering has been blamed on God, who supposedly wills it and even sends it. Suffering has led people away from God instead of bringing them to our suffering-with God as we know especially in Jesus crucified. Now, particularly in the light of liberation theology, we are understanding more and more that the lives of crucified peoples are continuations of Jesus' sufferings to bring about a new heaven and a new earth.

Salvadorian Jesuit theologians Ignacio Ellacuria and Jon Sobrino described El Salvador's suffering victims of war as crucified peoples. More recently, in *Christ the Liberator: A View from the Victims*, Sobrino has probed the mystery of suffering peoples in the context of Jesus' sufferings, an idea that resonates powerfully with Paul's testimony of continuing and completing the sufferings of Christ. In the introduction, Sobrino clarifies that the expression *victims* and the even stronger *crucified peoples* designate the challenge that has been indicated previously in the word *poor*.[7]

> Poverty, *first and foremost*, is the situation in which by far the greater part of the human race lives, bowed down under the weight of life. For these people,

survival is their greatest problem and death their closest destiny.[8]

In his challenging way, Sobrino then begins to probe the meaning of risen life in today's world, starting with theological developments beginning around the time of the Second Vatican Council. He reminds us that Jesus, "by rising as the firstborn," showed the way to the resurrection of all human beings.[9] Sobrino also indicates that the "coming of a new heaven and a new earth" is still more meaningful today when we speak of the cosmic Christ, whose power is at work in the entire universe.[10] However, the horrendous tragedies of today's crucified peoples, particularly the victims of war, cry out for further developments in our understanding and following of Jesus. Referring to a homily of Ellacuria in which he challenged young Jesuits to live as "risen beings in history," Sobrino insists that:

> . . . the following of Jesus can contain a sort of historical reverberation of his resurrection with two essential elements: (1) what there is of *fullness* in the resurrection, even in the midst of the limitations of history, and (2) what there is of *victory* in the resurrection against the enslavement of history.[11]

When we take an honest look at the urgent needs of survival in many of today's populations, the graphic images we encounter can give us a new meaning of the poor in the Gospels. The poor took special priority in Jesus' ministry; therefore, they must take special priority in the lives of us, Jesus' present-day disciples. In an article entitled "Remembering the Poor," Daniel Hartnett shares a recent interview with Gustavo Gutierrez, who explains that the urgency of response to the "subhuman condition" of poverty today "poses a major challenge to every Christian conscience and therefore to theology as well."[12] More recently, in a Lenten retreat at Loyola University Chicago, Gutierrez highlighted the significance and urgency of responding to the Church's recent call for basic structural changes in society today.

Our work for systemic changes in today's structural patterns—patterns that are making the rich richer and the poor poorer—truly calls for a stronger faith in the presence and power of the risen Jesus, who continues to send us the Befriending Spirit.

Our Moment of Supreme Crisis

When the Catholic bishops of the United States issued their pastoral letter "The Challenge of Peace," they reminded us that we are living in a "moment of supreme crisis."[13] In so doing, our bishops were quoting a key statement from the Second Vatican Council's teaching on "The Fostering of Peace and the Promotion of a Community of Nations" in *Gaudium et Spes*:

> In our generation when [people] continue to be afflicted by acute hardships and anxieties arising from the ravages of war or the threat of it, the whole

human family faces an hour of supreme crisis in its advance toward maturity. (GS 77)

How significant that our bishops used the phrase *supreme crisis*!

As the teaching in *Gaudium et Spes* continues, we are challenged to a peacemaking way of life. With the help of Christ, the Author of Peace, Christians are summoned "to cooperate . . . with [everyone] in securing among themselves a peace based on justice and love, and in setting up agencies of peace" (GS 77). The next section proclaims that peace is "the fruit of love, which goes beyond what justice can provide" (GS 78). Then this teaching of Vatican II relates our peace to our sharing in the life of our tripersonal God.

> That earthly peace which arises from love of neighbor symbolizes and results from the peace of Christ who comes forth from God the Father. For by His cross the incarnate Son, the Prince of Peace, reconciled all [people] with God. By thus restoring the unity of [everyone] in one people and one body, He slew hatred in His own flesh. After being lifted on high by His resurrection, He poured the Spirit of love into the hearts of [everyone]. (GS 78)

In pondering these prophetic texts from Vatican II, it is helpful to remember that the "Pastoral Constitution on the Church" was addressed not only to followers of Jesus Christ but to "the whole of humanity" (GS 2). Also we should emphasize that this conciliar teaching identified the "Spirit of love" as the "Befriending Spirit" (GS 3). Dependence on the Befriending Spirit was considered absolutely necessary for the "whole human family" in the hour of "supreme crisis" to face all the new complexities of family life, of economic, social and political questions, of modem warfare, of world-wide community.

In the very first article of *Gaudium et Spes*, the teaching on peace and the community of nations includes references to the Trinity, to the continual ways God shares divine tri-personal life with us. We are reminded that "earthly peace arises from love of neighbor," symbolizing and resulting "from the peace of Christ who comes forth from God the Father." By his suffering and death Jesus, the Prince of Peace, "slew hatred in His own flesh." Now, the risen Jesus pours "the Spirit of love into our hearts" (GS 78). In many ways these teachings of Vatican II echo the letter to the Ephesians. "He came and preached peace to you who were far off and peace to those who were near, for through him we both have access in one Spirit to the Father" (2:17).

These teachings of Vatican II point once again to Jesus' own promise of peace as proclaimed in the Eucharistic Discourse of John's Gospel. There, Jesus not only promises the gift of peace but also makes it unmistakably clear that his peace is a sharing of his divine life lived humanly (John 14:27). Throughout this conversation on the night of the Last Supper, Jesus refers to the relationship he enjoys with his Abba in the Holy Spirit. How beautiful that this climactic teaching of Jesus culminates in his prayer that we may share his oneness in love with his Father in their Holy Befriending Spirit. How pleadingly Jesus prays to his Abba "that the love with which you loved me may be in them and I in them" (John 17:26).

This Eucharistic Discourse is followed immediately by the Passion account of Jesus' suffering and death. Now more than ever, in our moment of supreme crisis, we face such excruciating sufferings of the people in our world and we need to see God's compassionate suffering-with love, not only in Jesus' passion and death but also in the crucified peoples all around us. Referring to Jesus' Eucharistic Discourse, *Gaudium et Spes* reminds us that Jesus "implied a certain likeness between the union of the divine Persons, and the unity of God's [children] in truth and charity" (GS 24). When we respond to suffering peoples in compassionate ways, we are, in essence, bringing forth new life because God's Befriending Spirit can be active through, with, and in *us*.

One historic response to the terrible oppression and violence of the twentieth century is the birth of international peace movements.[14] Each movement highlights the necessity of justice in the societal order if peace is to become a reality. Of special significance are three international peace movements begun by women: Women's International League of Peace and Freedom; Pax Christi, the international Catholic Peace Movement; and Global Peace Services, an interfaith effort. It is difficult to identify and measure the tremendous influence of these international movements. We might think of their impact in terms of two Gospel images, leaven and mustard seed, both seemingly insignificant while causing powerful change. Such movements are hopeful signs of the new creation process. Surely these peace movements are inspiring more ways to protest the violence of war. As James Lawson proclaimed recently in reference to the worldwide opposition to the war against Iraq:

> Unprecedented in human history, in the year 2003 . . . millions of people in 150 countries around the world took to the streets and cried NO TO WAR. Voices rang with the pathos of a profound human awareness that life means more than hatred or violence. Millions, perhaps billions, of human hearts all around the world are persuaded inwardly that life is meant for more than what we have made of the 21st century. Life is about truth and compassion. Life-giving activity. Life-creating possibilities.
>
> This march of millions is a phenomenon unmatched in either ancient or modem history.[15]

If *Gaudium et Spes* had been written at the beginning of this new millennium, surely the ecological concerns of our suffering world would have been added to the crucial issues facing us today in our moment of supreme crisis. In an article entitled "Biodiversity and the Holy Trinity" Belden Lane highlights the almost unimaginable variety of the millions of species God has created.[16] Lane reminds us that "we are now in a profoundly significant period of mass extinction."[17]

> The resultant spiraling loss is not only an ecological crisis, but also a failure of human beings to celebrate

what God has made. It diminishes our capacity to show forth the luster of the Holy Trinity. The threat to biodiversity is a theological, even liturgical problem, reducing our potential as an interrelated family species to give glory to God.[18]

Lane refers to contemporary theologians Leonardo Boff, Elizabeth Johnson, and Jürgen Moltmann, who are giving new and needed insight into God's tripersonal life:

> They ask how the doctrine of the Trinity can maintain a creative tension between two principles—the validation of "difference" (honored in the separate integrity of the Trinity's members) and the realization of "interconnecting unity" (joining them in a love that spontaneously seeks ever new things to love). Learning to respect a diversity of species within the wholeness of a larger system, therefore, becomes a Trinitarian as well as an ecological question.[19]

Our Dancing God

In early theological thought describing the mystery of the Trinity, the Greek word *perichoresis* was used to describe the interpenetrating union of the tripersonal life of God. Mary Ann Fatula explains:

> Because they *are* the one same life, the Father, Son and Spirit are inseparable; where one is, all three are. The divine persons live in one another; they

are one another's home. To hint at this magnificent truth, Latin writers used the word *circumincession*, "walking around" in one another. But the Greek theologians spoke instead of *perichoresis*, "dancing around," a word that suggests the dynamic activity and excitement it is to be God dwelling in God: the divine persons not only live in one another but also "dance" in one another.[20]

In a recent article, "The Trinity Is Our Social Program: The Doctrine of the Trinity and the Shape of Social Engagement," Miroslav Volf also shared timely insight into *perichoresis*:

> But the resources of *perichoresis* for thinking about identity are as rich as for thinking about unity. For it suggests that divine persons are not simply interdependent and influence one another from outside, but are *personally interior* to one another.[21]

Sharing in the life of our dancing God can become evermore meaningful as we contemplate the experience of dancing. Whether the dancing involves two persons or a large number of dancers, there is a most beautiful oneness in movement. Each dancer is a unique, distinct person. Together the dancers experience the beauty of the dance. An ever greater union between and among the dancers determines the ever greater beauty in the dancing experience.

Volf continues his development of *perichoresis* with reference to the new creation, to the making of all things new:

The Crucified One is the new creation—the perfect enactment of the eternal love of the Triune God in the godless world (cf. Romans 5:6–11). More precisely, the Crucified One is the new creation as it enters into the present creation become old through the practice of injustice, deception, and violence in order to transform godless humanity into humanity made in the image of the Triune God.[22]

Then Volf raises a critical question about the new creation and suffering:

Will the new creation be present only in pain and never in joy? Clearly not. After the resurrection of Christ and the sending of the Spirit, the new creation is *coming* into the sinful world ever anew in the movement from the cross to the empty tomb, in the labor of love and its transformation into the dance of love.[23]

One way to understand our participation in this mystery of the *tripersonal, dancing* God is to enjoy both the loving, prayerful resting and the ongoing, outgoing movements of justice and peacemaking. Whether we rest in God or dance with God, we must rely upon, and respond to, the inspiration of the Befriending Spirit. Our resting and dancing in the Spirit unite us evermore closely with the risen Jesus who is continually making all things new in our agonized, suffering world.

Only in God can we know genuine love. When the writer of the first letter of John tried to express the reality of God he simply said, "God is love and whoever remains in love remains in God and God in [them]" (1 John 4:16).

Thus our relationship to God has been described as mutual abiding. We also speak of it as mutual indwelling— God in us, and us in God. Now we add to those terms dancing, in which we move as individuals yet in concert with God our Abba, Jesus, and the Befriending Spirit. Just as the three "personalities" of the Trinity abide and dwell, rest and move in and amongst one another, we are able to do the same. In our dancing or our dwelling, we participate in the tripersonal life of God.

One of the Eucharistic Prayers prepared by the International Commission on English in the Liturgy in entitled Jesus the Compassion of God. Therein we pray, "Let your Church be a living witness to truth and freedom, to justice and peace, that all people may be lifted up by the hope of a world made new."[24]

As people of God, we will continue to learn what it means to abide in the tripersonal life of God. We will continue to learn how to allow that abiding to translate into action that helps make the world new. We must not forget, however, that we have access to one powerful action that will enliven us in the Holy Spirit and thus help us as we live out our radical hope for the future. That action is the sacrament of the Eucharist.

Every Eucharist reminds us that we need continual nourishment in this life of loving. Every Eucharist sends us forth to share God's life of compassionate love, especially with those who are suffering. Every Eucharist enables us to experience some of the joy Jesus promised in his Last Supper Discourse. "I have told you this so that my joy may be in you and your joy may be complete" (John 15:11). Every Eucharist enables us to enjoy more fully a life of friendship with God and with one another. Every Eucharist joyfully celebrates our oneness in God's tripersonal loving through, with, and in Jesus. Every Eucharist enables us to share life more vibrantly with our loving tripersonal God who is continually making all things new.

Questions for Reflection

1 Meditate on one of the New Testament texts on *new creation*, then describe how this meditation might work out for you in practical terms.

2. In what ways have you noticed the work of the Holy Spirit in your faith community? How do you see that community interacting with Jesus and with God the Father?

3. What does it mean to you that we can take on some of the suffering of Jesus? What does the term "crucified peoples" mean to you, and why?

4. Do you think we are at a "moment of extreme crisis"? If so, what would you offer as evidence? How does your own interaction with the tripersonal God influence the way you respond to crisis in the world?

5. What is your response to the idea of our "dancing" God? How would you describe your own spiritual movement and resting, abiding, and dancing, in relation to the Trinity?

6. What do you see as the basis for radical Christian hope? Where do you go for spiritual resources to fuel this hope and to participate in God's renewing action in the world?

NOTES

Chapter 1: The Befriending Spirit

1. Further considerations of the Befriending Spirit's role in our lives are given in Carol Frances Jegen, *Restoring Friendship with God* (Collegeville, MN: Liturgical Press, 1989), 44–45, 58–59, 80–81.

2. John Navone, *Enjoying God's Beauty* (Collegeville, MN: Liturgical Press, 1999), 5.

3. In recent years, an international meeting of representatives from small Christian communities took place at Notre Dame University. What a life-giving experience it was to form friendships with Christians from all over the world and to experience this special gifting of the Befriending Spirit in the formation of prayerful, caring communities.

4. More than one Taizé chant invites the Holy Creator Spirit to come into our world now. The sustained repetition of the chant, sometimes in different languages, can serve as a mantra that continues in one's mind and heart long after the communal chanting.

5. For a more extended commentary of the Isaian Servant Songs see Carol Frances Jegen, *Jesus the Peacemaker* (Kansas City, MO: Sheed and Ward, 1986).

6. Karl Rahner, "Man as the Event of God's Free and Forgiving Self-Communication," chapter 4 in *Foundations of Christian Faith*, trans., William V. Dych (New York: Crossroad, 1984).

7. Catherine LaCugna, *God for Us* (San Francisco: Harper, 1991), 156. Mary Ann Fatula, "The Holy Spirit and Human Actualization through Love: The Contribution of Aquinas," *Theology Digest* 32:3 (1985).

8. Ignace de la Potterie and Stanislaus Lyonnet, *The Christian Lives by the Spirit* (Staten Island, NY: Alba House, 1971), 64.

9. Navone, 117.

Chapter 2: Jesus

1. The renowned biblical scholar Gerhard Von Rad has emphasized that the Servant of Yahweh is the prophet par excellence, whose actions are his most powerful words. Gerhard Von Rad, *The Message of the Prophets*, trans. D.M.G. Stalker (New York: Harper & Row, 1985), 218f.

2. The Isaian author responsible for the Servant Songs (Isaiah 42:1–9; 50:4–9; 52:13—53:12) is often referred to as Second Isaiah or Deutero-Isaiah. There are three different authors responsible for the Book of Isaiah. Cf. W. Zimmerli and J. Jeremias, *The Servant of God* (London: SCM Press, 1957).

3. Zimmerli and Jeremias, 43f.

4. This Servant text, taken from the third and last part of the book of Isaiah, summarizes the prophet-servant's ministry resulting from the Spirit's anointing.

5. Zimmerli and Jeremias, 85f.

6. Jon Sobrino, *Christology at the Crossroads* (Maryknoll, NY: Orbis, 1978), 184f.

7. Jon Sobrino, "The Crucified Peoples: Yahweh's Suffering Servant Today," *Concilium* (1990), 6.

8. A helpful summary of historical and theological perspectives of the Servant Songs is given in Bo Reichke's "God's Servant in Old and New Testaments" (*Theology Digest* 29:1 [1981], 43–46).

9. John Thompson, *Modern Trinitarian Perspectives* (Oxford: Oxford University Press, 1994), 23.

10. Thompson, 23.

11. Catherine Mowry LaCugna, "The Self-Communication of God in Christ and the Spirit," chapter 7 in *God for Us: The Trinity and Christian Life* (San Francisco: Harper, 1991), 209–41.

12. It can be helpful to consider why receiving the Eucharist has often been referred to as Holy Communion.

13. Thompson, 234–5.

14. Ibid., 217.

15. Jürgen Moltmann, *History and the Triune God* (New York: Crossroad, 1992), 119.

16. G. O'Collins, *The Tripersonal God* (New York: Paulist, 1999). O'Collins gives timely insight into the dialogical aspects of the word *Logos*. "John's Logos teaching opened the way for Christians not only to recognize the influence of the Logos beyond Christianity but also to dialog with non-Christian thinkers," 80.

17. Carol Frances Jegen, *Restoring Friendship with God* (Collegeville, MN: Liturgical Press, 1989).

18. Jürgen Moltmann, *The Crucified God* (New York: Harper & Row, 1974), English translation.

19. A photo of the statue, displayed at the Center for Women and Peace, Mundelein College, Chicago, served for me as a continual call for repentance.

Chapter 3: Jesus' Abba and Ours

1. Michael Downey, *Altogether Gift: A Trinitarian Spirituality* (Maryknoll, NY: Orbis, 2000). "In recent decades, persuasive cases have been made for refraining from calling God 'Father.' The problem, however, is not with the name 'Father.' The problem lies in not hearing the story in which the name 'Father' is given, and in not explaining the name clearly enough," 19. Also see George T. Montague, "Freezing the Fire: The Death of Relational Language," *America* (March 13, 1993).

2. Elizabeth Johnson, *Consider Jesus* (New York: Crossroad, 1994), 57. John Meier translates *Abba* as "my own dear Father" in his article "Are There Historical

Links between the Historical Jesus and the Christian Ministry?" *Theology Digest* 47:4 (2000).

3. Hermann Schalück, "The Trinitarian Structure of Discipleship," *Theology Digest* 48:1 (2001), 44.

4. Jürgen Moltmann, *History and the Triune God* (New Yrok: Crossroad, 1992). In his first chapter, "Patriarchal or Non-Patriarchal Talk of God?" he emphasizes, "The name Abba reveals the inner heart of the relationship between Jesus and God," 11.

5. Jon Sobrino, *Christology at the Crossroads* (Maryknoll, NY: Orbis, 1978), 157.

6. Sobrino, *Christology*, 224.

7. Sobrino, *Christology*, 228–9, quoting Moltmann, *The Crucified God*.

8. Downey, *Altogether Gifts*, 28.

9. Recently, the word *kindom* is sometimes substituted for the word *kingdom*. Although *kindom* does suggest a familial relation, it does not indicate necessarily the Gospel meaning proclaimed in the kingdom imagery Jesus used to highlight the universal reign of God's love.

10. Sobrino, *Christology*, 356.

11. When the Catholic bishops of the United States began the Campaign for Human Development, designed to alleviate some of the dire poverty in this country, they used the graphic description "the hellish cycle of poverty."

12. Today's challenge of "hope against hope" is highlighted by Sobrino in *Christ the Liberator* (Maryknoll, NY: Orbis, 2001), 36–45.

13. Donald Senior, "Jesus Most Scandalous Teaching," in *Biblical and Theological Reflections on the Challenge of Peace*, ed. John T. Pawlikowski and Donald Senior (Wilmington, DE: Glazier, 1984), 55f.

14. A video describing a compassionate-listening process is available from Mid-East Citizen Diplomacy, P.O. Box 17, Indianola, WA 98342. Also see Marshall B. Rosenberg, *Nonviolent Communication: A Language of Compassion* (DelMar, CA: Puddle Dancers Press, 1999).

15. John Paul II, "Message for World Peace Day," *America* (January 7–14, 2002).

16. "The Mystery of Sin," chapter 2 in Carol Frances Jegen, *Restoring Our Friendship with God* (Collegeville, MN: Liturgical Press, 1989).

17. Barbara Reid emphasizes, "As the Fourth Evangelist tells it, God did not send Jesus to die for our sins, nor is suffering sent by God as a test of faith or as punishment for sin (9:3; 11:4). In this Gospel, Jesus invites all into friendship with himself, God, and one another." "Puzzling Passages: John 11:3," *The Bible Today*, 41:6 (2003), 387.

Chapter 4: The Meaning of God as Tripersonal

1. For example, in reference to the philosophical person/ nature language of the Council of Chalcedon in AD 451, Sobrino comments, "If the Christological formula makes a statement that is universally valid at its core, then this means that it must be subsequently interpreted in different historical situations and cultures. . . . The Chalcedonian formula would cease to be true if it turned out that people merely repeated it," *Christology at the Crossroads* (Maryknoll, NY: Orbis, 1978), 341.

2. A brief explanation is given in the *Catechism of the Catholic Church* (Liguori, MO: Liguori Publications, 1994), article 251, 66.

3. A most helpful summary of Rahner's theology is given in William Dych's book *Karl Rahner*. In chapter 10, "The Trinity," Dych quotes Rahner: "God has given himself so fully in his absolute self-communication to the creature, that the 'immanent' Trinity becomes the Trinity of the 'economy of salvation,' and hence in turn the Trinity of salvation which we experience IS the immanent Trinity. This means that the Trinity of God's relationship to us IS the reality of God as he is IN himself: a trinity of persons" (Collegeville, MN: Litrugical Press, 1992), 149, quoting *Theological Investigations* 4, 69.

4. Gerald O'Collins has exerted considerable influence on the use of *tripersonal* through his book *The Tripersonal God*.

5. For insights into the Pauline usage of these prepositions, see *The Jerome Biblical Commentary*, vol. 2, ed. Raymond Brown, Joseph Fitzmyer, Roland Murphy (Englewood Cliffs, NJ: Prentice Hall, 1968), 822–23.

6. Sobrino comments, "The relationship of Jesus of Nazareth to the Father has a history, and hence I would maintain that Jesus is not only the Son of the Father but also the Way to the Father," *Christology*, 339.

7. Elizabeth Johnson, *She Who Is* (New York: Crossroad, 1992), 68.

8. Paul J. Wadell, "The Subversive Ethics of the Kingdom of God," *The Bible Today*, 41:1 (2003), 11.

9. John R. Donahue, "Biblical Perspectives on Justice," *Faith That Does Justice*, ed. John Haughey (New York: Paulist, 1977), 69.

10. The freeing process of forgiveness is highlighted in Avis Clendenen and Troy Martin, *Forgiveness: Finding Freedom through Reconciliation* (New York: Crossroad, 2002).

11. John Paul II, "Message for World Peace Day," *America* (January 7–14, 2002).

Chapter 5: Making All Things New

1. Eugene Maly in *The Jerome Biblical Commentary*, Vol. 1, ed. Raymond Brown, Joseph Fitzmyer, Roland Murphy (Englewood Cliff, NJ: Prentice Hall, 1968) 7.

2. This tendency toward rebellion against God's design and the glorification of human ego and effort are understood in Christian theology to be the nature of sin itself, as lived out first of all in Adam and Eve's actions. A brief commentary on "original sin" is given in Jegen, *Restoring Our Friendship with God* (Collegeville, MN: Liturgical Press, 1989), 51–56.

3. Jürgen Moltmann, *History and the Triune God* (New York: Crossroad, 1992) ,119.

4. In the chapter "The Trinity and Worship" John Thompson states, "In other words, the triune God, who is in action for our salvation, is concerned not simply with human beings but with the renewal of the whole created order and with us as his instruments in that service." John Thompson, *Modern Trinitarian Perspectives* (Oxford: Oxford University Press, 1994), 101.

5. Hermann Schalück, "The Trinitarian Structure of Discipleship," *Theology Digest* 48:1, 47.

6. Carol Frances Jegen, "World Peace: Eucharistic Challenge," *Chicago Studies* (August 1980), 206f.

7. Jon Sobrino, *Christ the Liberator: A View from the Victims* (Maryknoll, NY: Orbis, 2001), 4f.

8. Sobrino, *Liberator*, 4.

9. Sobrino, *Liberator*, 11.

10. Sobrino, *Liberator*, 11.

11. Sobrino, *Liberator*, 13.

12. Daniel Hartnett, "Remembering the Poor," *America* (February 3, 2003).

13. This letter is both an invitation and a challenge to Catholics in the United States to join with others in shaping the conscious choices and deliberate policies required in this "moment of crisis." "The Challenge of Peace," United States Catholic Conference, Washington, DC (1983), 4.

14. For a brief description of the founding experiences of two peace movements, the Fellowship of Reconciliation and Pax Christi, see Mary Evelyn Jegen, "Theology and Spirituality of Nonviolence," *Worship*, vol. 60, no. 2 (March 1986), 124–125.

15. James Lawson, "Justice and Nonviolence in the Global Community," *Call to Action Spirituality Justice Reprint* (November/December, 2003).

16. Belden C. Lane, "Biodiversity and the Holy Trinity," *America*(December 17, 2001), 20.

17. Lane, "Biodiversity," 8.

18. Lane, "Biodiversity," 8.

19. Lane, "Biodiversity," 10.

20. Mary Ann Fatula, *The Triune God of Christian Faith* (Collegeville, MN: Liturgical Press, 1990), 67. See also Moltmann, *History*, 59, 131–132.

21. Miroslav Volf, "The Trinity Is Our Social Program: The Doctrine of the Trinity and the Shape of Social Engagement" (*Modern Theology* 14:3 July 1998), 409.

22. Volf, "Trinity," 418.

23. Volf, "Trinity," 418.

24. *Eucharistic Prayer for Masses* (Collegeville, MN: Liturgical Press, 1994), 42–50.

BIBLIOGRAPHY

The following books give extended background on recent developments in Trinitarian theology.

De la Potterie, Ignace, and Stanislaus Lyonnet. *The Christian Lives by the Spirit*. Staten Island, NY: Alba House, 1971.

Downey, Michael. *Altogether Gift: A Trinitarian Spirituality*. Maryknoll, NY: Orbis, 2000.

Drilling, Peter. *Trinity and Ministry*. Minneapolis, MN: Fortress Press, 1991.

Dych, William. *Karl Rahner*. Collegeville, MN: Liturgical Press, 1992. See especially chapter 10, "The Trinity."

Edwards, Denis. *The God of Evolution: A Trinitarian Theology*. New York: Paulist Press, 1999.

Fatula, Mary Ann. *The Triune God of Christian Faith*. Collegeville, MN: Liturgical Press, 1990.

Jegen, Carol Frances. *Jesus the Peacemaker*. Kansas City, MO: Sheed and Ward, 1986.

———. *Restoring Our Friendship with God*. Collegeville, MN: Liturgical Press, 1989.

Johnson, Elizabeth. *Consider Jesus*. New York: Crossroad, 1994.

———. *She Who Is*. New York: Crossroad, 1992.

LaCugna, Catherine Mowry. *God for Us: The Trinity and Christian Life*. San Francisco: Harper, 1991.

Moltmann, Jürgen. *History and the Triune God*. New York: Crossroad, 1992.

Navone, John. *Enjoying God's Beauty*. Collegeville, MN: Liturgical Press, 1999.

O'Collins, Gerald. *The Tripersonal God: Understanding and Interpreting the Trinity*. New York: Paulist, 1999.

Rahner, Karl. *Foundations of Christian Faith*. Trans. William V. Dych. New York: Crossroad, 1984.

Sobrino, Jon. *Christology at the Crossroads*. Maryknoll, NY: Orbis, 1978.

———. *Christ the Liberator: A View from the Victims*. Maryknoll, NY: Orbis, 2001.

Thompson, John. *Modern Trinitarian Perspectives*. Oxford: Oxford University Press, 1994.

Thompson, William M. *The Struggle for Theology's Soul*. New York: Crossroad Herder, 1996.